To our colleague, John Iliff,

Your dedication to innovation in
libraries continues to inspire.

Know that you are missed.

Table of Contents

Dedication   iii

List of Figures   ix

Preface   xi

1. **RSS Creator: A Journal Table of Contents
   Alerting Service**   1
   David Walker

   Abstract   1
   About the Author   1
   Introduction   1
   Problems with Existing E-mail Table of Contents Alerts
       and Journal RSS Feeds   2
   RSS Creator   5
       Benefits of RSS Creator   10
       Challenges of RSS Creator   11
       Conclusion   12
       References   13

2. **Currency, Convenience, and Context: RSS
   Applied to Subscription Database Content**   17
   John Law

   Abstract   17
   About the Author   17
   Introduction   18
   RSS for Subscription Databases   19
       RSS Applications   20
       The Subscription Database Platform   22

v

The Integration of RSS Feeds into Web Pages 25
Value to the Library Mission 26
Users, RSS Readers, and Self-Aggregation 28
Custom Library Services 29
Potential Issues 32
Future Uses 33
Conclusion 34
References 35

3. **Wiki as Research Guide** 39
Chad Boeninger

Abstract 39
About the Author 39
Introduction 39
The Need for Change 41
Setting Up the Wiki 43
The Biz Wiki's Content 45
The Biz Wiki's Organization and Search Features 47
Adding and Editing Content 49
Measuring Usage of the Biz Wiki 52
Challenges 52
Conclusion 54
References and Further Reading 54

4. **Library Blogs: The New Technology
Bandwagon** 59
Steven J. Bell

Abstract 59
About the Author 59
Introduction 60
Do Your Users Want A Library Blog? Can They Use It? .. 62
A Better Way to Blog to Your Community 64
RSS to Javascript Converters 64
A Student Experiment 69
Reactions to Blogging to Courseware 70

vi

Tips for Successful Library Blogging 71
    Update Regularly 72
    Quality Content 72
    Quick Completion 73
    Content Policies 73
    Review Library Blogs 73
Unforeseen Benefits 74
Conclusion 75
2006 Survey Questions and Response Data 76
References 80

5. **An Introduction to Podcasting for Librarians** 83
John Iliff and Tyler Rousseau

Abstract 83
About the Authors 83
Introduction 84
Understanding Podcasts 85
Podcasting Today 85
    Finding Podcasts 85
    Who Is Listening? 86
    Who Is Podcasting? 87
Creating a Podcast 88
    Recording the Audio File: Computer and Microphone . . 88
    Recording the Audio File: Public Address System . . . 89
    Editing the Audio File 91
    Incorporating Multiple Audio Files 91
    Saving the Audio File 92
    Creating the RSS Feed 93
Validating the RSS Feed 94
    Library Podcasts 94
Conclusion 97
References and Further Reading 97

Index 99
About the Editors 105

vii

List of Figures

Figure 1.1: Search Results from RSS Creator 6
Figure 1.2: Full Record Display in RSS Creator
             with Related Journals 7
Figure 1.3: RSS Creator Creates a Feed in Real Time 8
Figure 1.4: RSS Creator Technical Infrastructure 9
Figure 1.5: Subscribed Feeds in a User's Desktop
             Aggregator 10

Figure 2.1: Illustration of Predefined Topical RSS
             Feeds 22
Figure 2.2: Illustration of Results Page Link for Creating
             a Custom RSS Feed 23
Figure 2.3: Illustration of Setup Page for a Custom
             RSS Feed 24
Figure 2.4: Illustration of URL and Confirmation Page
             for a Custom RSS Feed 24
Figure 2.5: System Diagram for ProQuest Custom
             RSS Feeds 25
Figure 2.6: Sample HTML Page Displaying RSS Feed
             Contents 27
Figure 2.7: Online Survey of ProQuest End Users,
             March 2006 29
Figure 2.8: Library E-resources Page with RSS Feeds
             Integration 30
Figure 2.9: Faculty Page with RSS Feeds Integration
             on the Right 31
Figure 2.10: College Department Web Page with RSS
             Feeds Integration on the Right 32

Figure 3.1:   Biz Wiki Article for Demographics USA   46
Figure 3.2:   Biz Wiki Article for SWOT Analysis   47
Figure 3.3:   Categories in the Biz Wiki   49
Figure 3.4:   The Web-based Interface   50
Figure 3.5:   Creating Wiki Content during a Reference
              Transaction   51
Figure 3.6:   Popular Pages in the Biz Wiki   53

Figure 4.1:   Entering the URL of the RSS Feed   65
Figure 4.2:   Options from the Feed2JS Converter   66
Figure 4.3:   The Javascript Code   67
Figure 4.4:   The Pasted Javascript Code   67
Figure 4.5:   The Finished Announcements Page   68
Figure 4.6:   Paul J. Gutman Library Home Page
              Showing Blog   68

Figure 5.1:   Juice Page Showing Several Subscriptions
              and the Recent Contents of One Podcast . . .   86
Figure 5.2:   A Single Vocal Track on Audacity   90
Figure 5.3:   A Musical Track Fading Out Behind
              an Original Vocal Track   92
Figure 5.4:   Feed Validation   94
Figure 5.5:   Omnibus   95
Figure 5.6:   Click-A-Story   96

Preface

In *Using Interactive Technologies in Libraries: A LITA Guide,*
leading professionals introduce you to some of today's most
promising high-tech library applications. You may be familiar with
the idea of a "hype cycle." When a new technology emerges, high
expectations initially create a growing positive reaction, or "hype."
Many of the topics in this book may be approaching the height of
their hype cycles. The word "podcasting" was selected as the
word of the year for 2005 by the New American Oxford Dictionary. Blogs, blogging, and bloggers are all over the media. Amid
such enthusiasm, librarians must learn where the hype stops and
reality begins.

Each chapter in *Using Interactive Technologies in Libraries*
presents in-depth, practical information written by an author who
has had real-world success. The authors will show you how to determine whether to implement a particular technology. If you
decide to use it, you will learn how to make the most of your new
endeavor. They will help you see through the buzz to determine
the most useful applications.

Libraries have been at the forefront of adoption of RSS—Really
Simple Syndication. Given the interest in the topic, the first two
chapters of this volume focus on this exciting means of information
distribution. In Chapter 1, "RSS Creator: A Journal Table of Contents Alerting Service," David Walker describes how he provides
an integrated alerting service for journal contents through RSS.
David's approach to content syndication takes awareness services
to a new level. He uses metasearch and OpenURL-based technology to supply information based on disciplinary interests across

vendor platforms. His example represents a truly thoughtful and effective way of using an innovation to add value to library services.

In Chapter 2, "Currency, Convenience, and Context: RSS Applied to Subscription Database Content," John Law offers a vendor perspective on RSS as applied to subscription database content. After a brief overview of the technology and its context, John shows how libraries can use the RSS search feeds now offered by content providers such as ProQuest. Search feeds can filter based on publication, on predefined criteria, or on custom criteria defined by the library. These simple yet powerful examples illustrate the many potential uses of these feeds in libraries.

Chapter 3, "Wiki as Research Guide," offers a useful example for using Wiki software to provide enhanced services to patrons. Chad Boeninger of Ohio University describes his experiences creating a business research Wiki. Librarians have been producing subject guides almost as long as there have been librarians, but moving the traditional print-based subject guide to the Web has been fraught with issues. As Chad points out, traditional methods of creating subject guides on the Web have relied on static HTML pages. This method requires people to have web-authoring skills and suffers from inflexibility in authoring methods. But by using Wiki-based software to create guides like Chad's "The Biz Wiki," we can update subject guides instantly and better meet patron needs.

Steven Bell provides a constructive look at blog use in courseware in Chapter 4, "Library Blogs: The New Technology Bandwagon." As Steven notes, there is often pressure to implement new technology. When considering a new idea, librarians need to ask if the result is actually useful for patrons. Here is a useful outline for how to use blog feeds within courseware to reach students with fresh and dynamic library-related content. Applying blogs in this way positions the library as a significant contributor to the learning process.

Finally, John Iliff and Tyler Rousseau discuss podcasting in Chapter 5, "An Introduction to Podcasting for Librarians." John and Tyler provide a context and look at potential podcasting issues. They examine the role libraries will play in this new media environment. John and Tyler look toward the future by highlighting some library efforts in this area. The editors are certain that John Iliff would have been pleased that the organization for which he worked is now making effective use of podcasting in their new series, PALINET's Technology Conversations Podcast Series, available at http://www.palinet.org/rss/tech-conversations. The editors would also like to thank Tyler Rousseau for taking over authorship of this chapter after John Iliff's passing and Karen Iliff, John's widow, for facilitating this process. His contribution to the profession is lasting.

Librarians strive to organize the entire store of recorded human knowledge, but the format and nature of information is constantly changing. From cuneiform tablets through printed books to constantly changing Internet information, the trend is toward greater participation in the creation and distribution of the body of knowledge. The Web makes available the power of a printing press, radio station, and film studio to anyone with a computer and an idea. Librarians should endeavor to understand each new technology as it comes along and, ideally, learn how to use it themselves. Enjoy the varied perspectives and examples represented in these chapters. Readers may feel free to contact the editors with any questions or comments relating to this guide.

Kathlene Hanson
Electronic Resources Coordinator
California State University Monterey Bay
kathlene_hanson@csumb.edu

H. Frank Cervone
Assistant University Librarian for Information Technology
Northwestern University
f-cervone@northwestern.edu

Chapter 1

RSS Creator: A Journal Table of Contents Alerting Service

David Walker

Abstract

This chapter describes RSS Creator, an open source journal table of contents alerting service developed at California State University San Marcos using the Metalib X server and SFX link resolver. The author examines the limitations of current table of contents alerting systems and publisher-supplied RSS feeds; the technical details of RSS Creator; and the scale, cost, and maintenance advantages of developing an open source table of contents system.

About the Author

David Walker is Web Development Librarian at California State University San Marcos. His work centers on the integration and customization of library information systems, with a focus on interface design and metasearch.

Introduction

In recent years, technology experts have heralded Really Simple Syndication (RSS) as an innovative step forward in the sharing of information over the Web. A lightweight XML standard for syndicating news and other timely content, RSS has the potential to replace many current Web and e-mail-based applications. As

Internet users increasingly look to filter and personalize their interactions on the Web, RSS has the potential to become an essential part of the average user's daily life.

If there is a use for RSS in academic libraries, journal tables of contents would be an obvious first choice. Journals provide content that is timely, periodic, and of great interest to faculty and other researchers. This is precisely the type of information RSS was designed to syndicate. Many libraries currently use commercial e-mail-based table of contents alerting systems, which could be replaced by RSS-based systems.

This chapter looks at these issues in greater depth, examining the limitations of current table of contents alerting systems and publisher-supplied RSS feeds, and the advantages of developing an open source table of contents system. Throughout the chapter, the author will reference RSS Creator, an open source journal table of contents alerting service originally developed at California State University San Marcos using the Metalib X server and SFX link resolver.

Problems with Existing E-mail Table of Contents Alerts and Journal RSS Feeds

Since at least the 1960s, libraries have sought ways to systematically inform their users of new content. Large research libraries in particular have long offered table of contents services to faculty and researchers, initially through print distribution and more recently via e-mail and other network tools (Cox and Hanson, 1992). Manually creating such lists and locally managing e-mail subscriptions is time-consuming and labor-intensive. Some libraries direct users to individual e-mail subscription services available through various database providers, but it can be difficult for users to discover and utilize such services when they are scattered among several different sites. Other libraries have purchased commercial alerting services to consolidate these alerts into a single point of entry, and at least one elite academic library has built a homegrown system for this purpose (Horne and Kristensen,

2004). E-mail has proven to be a rather inflexible medium for integration, and smaller college libraries have neither the money for a commercial system nor the staff resources to build such a system locally. As users find their e-mail inboxes increasingly difficult to manage, offloading journal content alerts to systems other than e-mail becomes more desirable.

Moving from e-mail to RSS-based table of contents alerts can solve some of these problems, and can also open up the possibility for libraries and library end users to take advantage of the flexible nature of XML to repurpose these tables of contents, or portions thereof, in different contexts and systems, such as student e-portfolios, campus portals, or learning management systems. However, there are a number of problems with the current state of publisher-supplied and database provider-supplied RSS feeds.

First, few publishers or database providers currently offer RSS feeds. Some publishers, such as Oxford University Press, have made their feeds publicly available, and some libraries have started putting together lists of publicly available RSS feeds, the largest of which include only a few hundred titles. Some database providers, such as EbscoHost and Proquest, have begun offering RSS feeds for both saved searches and journal table of contents alerts. However, these new RSS services remain the exception rather than the rule. Database providers are still working out how best to authenticate users who subscribe to these feeds, an important challenge that will be discussed in greater detail below.

Second, much like the e-mail alerting services currently available from some publishers and database providers, publisher-supplied feeds must be discovered, collected, and maintained by libraries in order to maximize their availability. Without this necessary task, the feeds will remain scattered across dozens of Web sites, making them difficult for users to find or use. Users will need to navigate each Web site's unique (and oftentimes cumbersome) interface in order to locate the feeds. In the case of database providers, users will need to establish an account and remember a

3

unique login in order to gain access to the feeds. Collecting, storing, compiling, and updating journal RSS feeds would greatly facilitate access, but it is a task that requires significant ongoing work, including all of the problems of link maintenance, made doubly difficult in the ever-shifting world of electronic journals.

Finally, and most importantly, publisher-supplied RSS feeds link directly back to the publisher's Web site, bypassing library proxy servers and link resolvers. The very purpose of RSS is to offer content publishers a mechanism for the centralized dissemination of information. A content provider can make one XML file available to all potential users, which greatly simplifies content syndication and subscription management. RSS was conceived and designed for the open Web, where users access free Web sites and blogs or gain access to premium content using personal subscriptions. RSS assumes a direct relationship between publisher and subscriber. This model does not hold true in libraries, where users gain access to subscription content by virtue of their affiliation with a university or public library, which serves as an intermediary between publishers and users.

Here, then, we have something of a conflict in technology. A graduate student at California State University San Marcos may have access to some of the content provided by a publisher's Web site by virtue of her affiliation with the university, and may even be able to subscribe to an RSS feed from the publisher. But if the student accesses the feed from outside of the campus IP range, or the library does not have online full-text access for that particular journal—or, worse, has full-text access via a different database—the publisher-supplied RSS feed offers the student no way to access the actual journal article itself. The link for each article will simply take him or her back to the publisher's Web site, where the student will be asked to log in or told that his or her institution does not have access. The library may have a print subscription to the journal, and certainly can secure a copy through interlibrary loan, but those are not options available to the student through an RSS feed or from a publisher's Web site.

RSS Creator

Given the problems inherent in publisher-supplied RSS feeds, a better approach is needed. RSS Creator, a project started at California State University San Marcos, provides just such a new approach. It is a server application and Web interface designed using Microsoft's .Net framework and allows a library to utilize its subscription databases together with Ex Libris' SFX link resolver and MetaLib metasearch systems to discover, create, and maintain journal RSS feeds. Through this process, a library can design a table of contents alerting service for its local users in a way that takes into account the unique nature of library subscriptions and authentication mechanisms.

There are three steps in the process. The first step is for a library to download its journal subscription information out of the SFX Knowledgebase. This can include only those journals that the library subscribes to in full text, but since SFX also maintains information about which journals are simply indexed and abstracted in each database, a library can choose to include this wider set of journals as well. In this way, smaller college libraries can provide table of content alerts for journals beyond their immediate collection, which is usually aimed at supporting the undergraduate curriculum. Given that table of contents alerts are likely to be of interest only to faculty and graduate students, this ability to offer alerts for journals in the faculty's areas of research is an important goal of the system. A library can choose to export the data using SFX's simple export utilities, which can produce a tab-delimited file containing the minimal set of information (title, ISSN, and coverage dates) for each journal, or, optionally, with Ex Libris' MARCit service, enhance this information with CONSER MARC records, giving a fuller set of metadata. San Marcos has chosen the latter approach in order to provide more robust search and discovery options.

After downloading the MARC records in MARC-XML format from SFX, the second step in the process is for the library to upload this file to RSS Creator. Using Lucene, the popular open

5

source indexing library, RSS Creator processes and indexes journals that have open-ended holdings—in other words, journals that continue to be published (Figure 1.1). After RSS Creator indexes the entire collection of journals, it performs a second run through the collection, associating similar journal titles based on Library of Congress subject headings. From the library's Web site, users can then search RSS Creator for journals by keyword, title, subject, or other fields deemed important by the library, with results sorted by relevance or title (Figure 1.2). In the full record display of each journal, RSS Creator uses the associated journal title information to offer users "more like this." In this way, users can search and browse the collection.

When a user chooses to subscribe to an alert for a journal, RSS Creator checks to see if it has previously created a feed for another

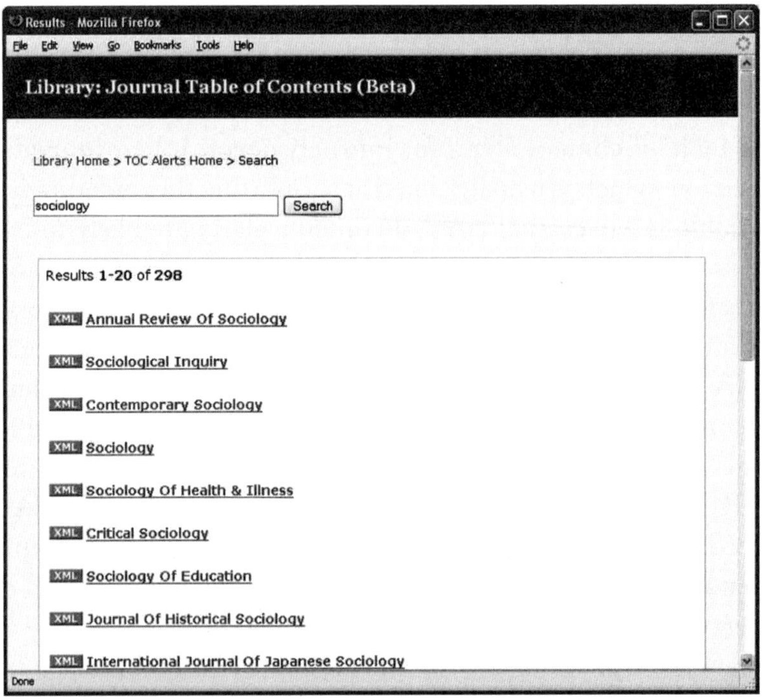

Figure 1.1: Search Results from RSS Creator

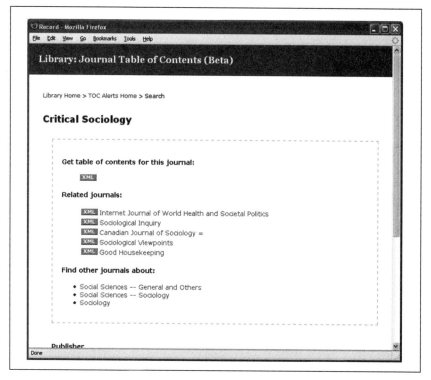

Figure 1.2: Full Record Display in RSS Creator with Related Journals

user. If this is the first time someone has selected a feed, RSS Creator sends an ISSN query to the database that indexes that journal via the Metalib X server, a Web services API to the Metalib metasearch system (Figure 1.3). Metalib, in turn, searches the selected database, pulling the articles for that journal in reverse chronological order. MetaLib then normalizes the data from the source database to an internal MARC format, parsing the records and creating an OpenURL Context Object from the information available in each record based on rules defined in the MetaLib Knowledgebase. The Metalib X server then serializes both the original MARC record and the OpenURL data to XML, sending that back to RSS Creator. RSS Creator continues to pull records from Metalib until it has reached the end of the current issue, transforms the MARC-XML to RSS, and creates an OpenURL link for each article, which points to San

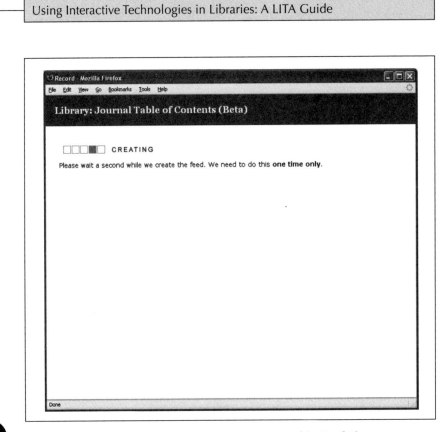

Figure 1.3: RSS Creator Creates a Feed in Real Time

Marcos' SFX link resolver (Figure 1.4). Subsequent users who select the feed are sent to a locally cached copy. A scheduled task updates the feeds on a regular basis.

Once RSS Creator provides the user with a feed, he or she can then add it to a desktop or browser, their e-mail, or a Web-based RSS aggregator (Figure 1.5). This application then takes care of presenting the feed to the user in a human-readable way, highlighting unread articles, and periodically querying the feed location for new content. Users can choose to keep old articles in their aggregator as long as they like, delete ones they no longer want, filter results by keyword, and use other features. Leveraging existing RSS aggregators and shifting the presentation of feed information to client applications greatly simplifies the development and delivery of a table of contents alerting service. By using the existing

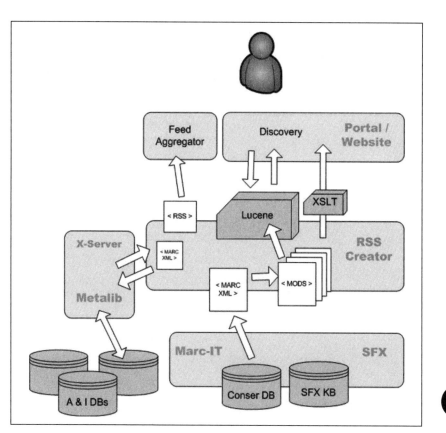

Figure 1.4: RSS Creator Technical Infrastructure

RSS infrastructure in this fashion, California State San Marcos was able to develop RSS Creator far more quickly than if the library had to develop this mechanism from scratch.

Indeed, the central goal of the project was to create a system that required very little staff time to set up and maintain. By utilizing the library's current subscription databases and commercial library systems, as well as leveraging the open standards of RSS and free client aggregators, California State San Marcos was able to create a table of contents alerting service at no cost beyond development time. The monthly maintenance of exporting the SFX knowledge-base takes less than five minutes. RSS Creator indexes, creates, and updates the feeds automatically.

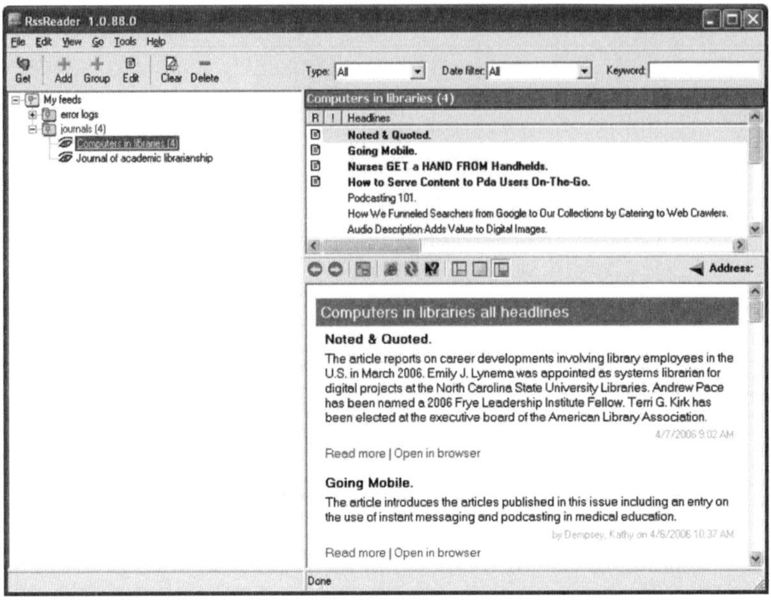

Figure 1.5: Subscribed Feeds in a User's Desktop Aggregator

Benefits of RSS Creator

RSS Creator provides several benefits that publisher-supplied RSS feeds do not. First of all, it gives a library instant access to 20,000–40,000 or more feeds, depending on the size and scope of the library's database subscriptions. The system can create feeds for virtually any journal or newspaper indexed in a library's subscription database, so long as that database is searchable via Metalib, regardless of whether the publisher or database provider makes feeds available.

Second, it almost entirely eliminates the need for discovery, collection, and maintenance of feeds. Instead of the feeds being scattered among various Web sites or manually collected by the library, all of the information necessary to create the feeds is already available in the SFX Knowledgebase. A library simply downloads this information out of SFX and uploads it into RSS Creator. RSS Creator takes care of the creation and maintenance of the feeds themselves. All of the feeds are in one place and are conveniently available to library users on the library's Web site.

Finally, all links point back to the library's link resolver. RSS Creator simply creates an OpenURL for each article title, which, in the case of California State San Marcos, links the user to the library's SFX menu. If a faculty member sees a journal article they want to read, regardless of whether they are on campus or not, SFX will provide them proxied access to the full text, provide information about print availability in the library, or even provide a pre-populated ILL form if San Marcos does not have access to the article online or in print.

Challenges of RSS Creator

Despite the many benefits of RSS Creator, there are some unique challenges with this particular approach. First of all, there is overlap and variability in the indexing of journals among the various databases. Three or four databases in a library's subscription might index the same journal. Should the library provide separate feeds for each source? If only one database is selected to serve as the source of the feed, which one should it be, and how would a library select it? Some databases selectively index journals. Sociological Abstracts from CSA, for example, includes a core set of journals which are indexed and abstracted completely, but also a second tier of journals, the articles of which are included only when the database editors deem them relevant. RSS Creator could very easily create feeds for these selective titles, but their inclusion in a table of contents alerting service would be misleading, giving the false impression that they were complete.

Second, the SFX Knowledgebase is not completely comprehensive, particularly for journals that are only indexed in a database and not available in full text. The ability to link from a citation to the full text of a journal is the marquee feature of any OpenURL link resolver, and Ex Libris naturally focuses its efforts on tracking full-text titles. Database providers who accurately report their non-full-text titles, such as EbscoHost, are well represented in the

11

knowledgebase, but several database providers that California State University San Marcos subscribes to are not. The library is exploring ways to include those titles into SFX in a cost-effective manner. Another problem is that the SFX Knowledgebase itself contains only minimal data for each journal. The Ex Libris MARCit service is a real benefit in this regard, since it can flesh out the records with a fuller set of data, but there is not always a CONSER record for each title. In testing at San Marcos, MARCit was unable to provide enhanced MARC data for roughly 3% of the journals.

Finally, there is the challenge of instructing faculty about RSS itself. Although the standard is quickly being adopted in a number of new applications, it has not yet reached full maturity. Downloading and learning a new application can be a real barrier to casual computer users, and teaching users how to recognize and manually add feeds to an aggregator proves to be another barrier as well. Faculty members are particularly hard to track down and instruct on new technology. Therefore, the greatest challenge for RSS Creator might be social rather than technical in nature. The library at San Marcos has begun offering workshops to faculty on the new system, with more advertising and awareness campaigns planned for the future. Full-scale adoption of RSS and the real potential of a system like RSS Creator may not be realized until subscribing to an RSS feed becomes a seamless experience. The next generation of Web browsers—in particular Internet Explorer 7—will go a long way toward making this a reality.

Conclusion

As a lightweight XML format for the exchange of information, RSS holds out great promise for the sharing and repurposing of content. Libraries face a number of unique challenges in utilizing RSS, particularly since the architecture of RSS assumes a direct relationship between content publishers and subscribers, while libraries serve as intermediaries between publishers and users. RSS Creator addresses these fundamental challenges by leveraging existing library systems and databases to create feeds locally and by utilizing key library standards, including OpenURL, and widely adopted technology, such as proxy servers, to ensure seamless access to the full text of articles.

References

Cox, John, and Terry Hanson. 1992. Setting Up an Electronic Current Awareness Service. *Online* 16 (4):36–43.

Horne, Angelina K., and Terry L. Kristensen. 2004. The Development of MyContents, and Enriched Electronic Table of Contents Service. *Portal: Libraries & the Academy* 4 (2):205–18.

13

Notes

Notes

Currency, Convenience, and Context: RSS Applied to Subscription Database Content

John Law

Abstract

RSS is being widely adopted throughout the online community and is firmly taking root in library applications. This elegant technology takes advantage of existing infrastructures and standards to enable seamless, automatic transfer of content across domains for integration with library and patron applications. This chapter describes new RSS services being made available for subscription research databases. Librarians can leverage these capabilities to enhance libraries' online presence and the patron's experience in the library.

17

About the Author

As director of tactical alliances and platform development at ProQuest Information and Learning, John Law manages the ProQuest online search engine platform. He is responsible for strategic planning, user research, and definition of new features and technologies for the platform such as ProQuest® Smart Search, as well as interoperability capabilities such as support for OpenURL and federated search applications. John writes and speaks at industry conferences on topics related to technology, user-centered design of applications, and product development, both from a library market perspective and in relation to new products management practices. John holds a Bachelor's degree in engineering from Michigan State University and a Master's degree focused on technology management from Columbia University.

Introduction

While overwhelming amounts of content are easily searched online both inside and outside of the library, the task of finding and keeping abreast of relevant new content is burdensome and overwhelming to researchers, students, and faculty members, especially in terms of time efficiency and productivity. Libraries, already taking advantage of online research databases, have opportunities to advance further in serving the needs of their patrons by employing RSS-based solutions for packaging and delivering this content.

Using RSS, librarians now have the ability to make premium content available precisely in context for their patrons. For example, focused streams of licensed content can be made available on various topic-oriented library and campus sites, providing the most recent relevant content at sites users frequent. RSS can enrich the research experience, adding value and efficiency. Other scenarios for using RSS in libraries include allowing patrons to create their own highly-focused customized content streams, bringing them highest-relevancy content as it becomes available, and allowing them to integrate this content into their local environment in a way best suited to their workflow.

In this chapter we will examine how RSS will become an integral element of licensed content delivery for both libraries and patrons; how RSS services are designed and used with these databases; and how RSS increases value across the entire content supply and consumption chain.

RSS for Subscription Databases

"Simplicity, simplicity, simplicity."

— Henry David Thoreau

"Everything should be made as simple as possible, but not simpler."

— Albert Einstein

"Simplification is one of the most difficult things to do."

— Jonathan Ive, Designer of the Apple iPod

RSS is an amazing new application of commonplace technology. Using standard Internet protocol and markup languages together with straightforward XML formatting rules, RSS allows for content to be easily aggregated from multiple sources or integrated into multiple services. It allows non-technical users to access, package, and present content in a highly customized fashion. The user only needs to do the initial site or service setup. The content is automatically updated and refreshed.

Application of RSS on the Web is increasing at an astonishing rate, and application in libraries and universities is quickly catching on. ProQuest is one of the first aggregators in the library market to utilize RSS feeds. Other content service providers that have introduced RSS feeds include PubMed, Engineering Village 2, and Factiva. RSS is an easy way for libraries to create valuable, in-context links to their subscription content while enhancing services to their users by integrating the latest articles in a particular field into the corresponding e-resources page on their library Web site.

Offering RSS feeds for subscription databases provides the following benefits

- Expands the exposure and accessibility of database content for libraries, their institutions, and patrons
- Increases the "embeddedness" of library resources in online environments, placing the content in context for users and increasing the prominence of the library in the user environment

19

- Increases usage of subscription databases, fostering an improved value proposition
- Enables customized selection of licensed content to be displayed at compelling points of use, including course sites and library subject pages
- Allows end users to subscribe to feeds of relevant articles based on their unique research topics and then have ongoing access feed conveniently from their RSS aggregator/reader (freely available on the Web) along with their other sources of research

Librarians are excited about the potential that RSS holds for increasing exposure of library resources, thereby improving the value proposition (and perception) of the library among their constituents. RSS enables the packaging of library resources into custom feeds tailored for particular audiences, topics, and applications. Placing access to library resources, packaged in this fashion, in various library and non-library Web spaces raises the profile of the library and their resources.

20

ProQuest offers freely available RSS feeds by subject for its PhD dissertation collection. There are feeds for about 30 subject areas in education, engineering, biological sciences, earth and environmental sciences, political sciences, sociology, and physics. A separate set of feeds tailored to business school curricula also is freely available.

RSS Applications

RSS, like other Web 2.0 technologies such as Ajax, is readily deployed because of its simplicity. This makes the technology extremely appealing. In broad strokes, here is how RSS feeds work with subscription databases

- The database user is presented with a link or button to subscribe to an RSS feed. A URL corresponding to the RSS feed is provided for the user to copy. The user adds the RSS URL to their Website or reader application.

- The user's application "visits" the Web page corresponding to the RSS URL and harvests the XML data provided by the subscription database, displaying the contents in the user's application interface

- Behind the scenes, the subscription database platform checks regularly for new content that corresponds to (matches the criteria for) the RSS feed selected by the user. Whenever new content is identified, the corresponding XML page for that feed is updated to include the content metadata. The date stamp on the page is updated to indicate that new content has been added to the page.

- On some frequent basis, the user's application revisits the RSS page to check for updates. If the date stamp on the page indicates the data has been updated since the last visit, the user's application harvests the new XML data and presents it in the user's application interface.

There are several different types of RSS feeds that apply to subscription databases. Predefined feeds as illustrated in Figure 2.1 below are created by the database provider and comprised of a set of topic-based feeds. Predefined feeds are extremely convenient for users to select, but the choices have a practical limit. Most RSS feeds available on the open Web are predefined.

Another popular type of RSS feed is a publication feed. Publication feeds are updated with each new issue of a publication, essentially providing a table of contents alerting service but in the form of a convenient XML feed for dynamically populating Web pages or personal RSS readers.

Last and perhaps most valuable, RSS feeds are just beginning to become available for custom searches. This type of feed is most similar to the now commonplace e-mail search alerts. For any search that can be defined and executed in the subscription database, the user can elect to create a corresponding RSS feed. In this

21

case the feed contents can be precisely focused on the area of research pertinent to the user's project.

The Subscription Database Platform

The implementation of RSS feeds at ProQuest has been relatively straightforward, requiring limited development resources and little incremental hardware capital investment. The initial application of RSS was in support of predefined topical feeds made available on the open Web for various database products. See Figure 2.1 as an example.

The implementation of support for custom RSS feeds, or RSS Search Alerts, is more complex. For this feature, a "Create RSS Feed" link is added to the search results page (see Figure 2.2).

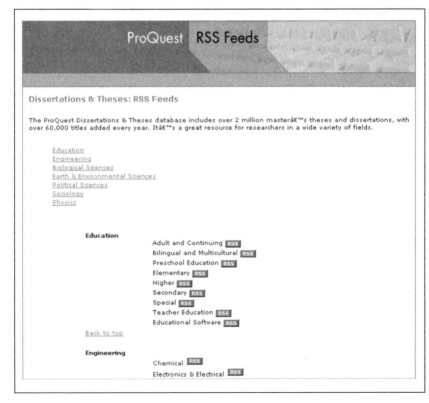

Figure 2.1: Illustration of Predefined Topical RSS Feeds

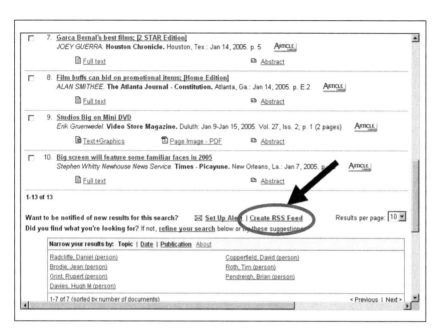

Figure 2.2: Illustration of Results Page Link for Creating a Custom RSS Feed

At this point, the user has constructed and executed a search. Provided the results are satisfactory and on target for their research, the user has the option then to elect to subscribe to an RSS feed for any new matching content added to the database in the future. To do so, the user clicks on the "Create RSS Feed" link. This link displays a setup page as illustrated in Figure 2.3.

The setup page allows the user to specify a name for their alert, verify the search parameters, and specify an e-mail address so that the URL corresponding to the RSS feed can be e-mailed to them for future reference. Clicking "Create" displays a URL representing the location where the RSS-compliant XML formatted search alert will ultimately be available (see Figure 2.4).

The design solution for supporting this feature extends an existing proprietary e-mail search alerts software application. See an illustrative diagram of the design solution in Figure 2.5.

The alerting application software module checks daily for any new content matching search criteria associated with custom RSS

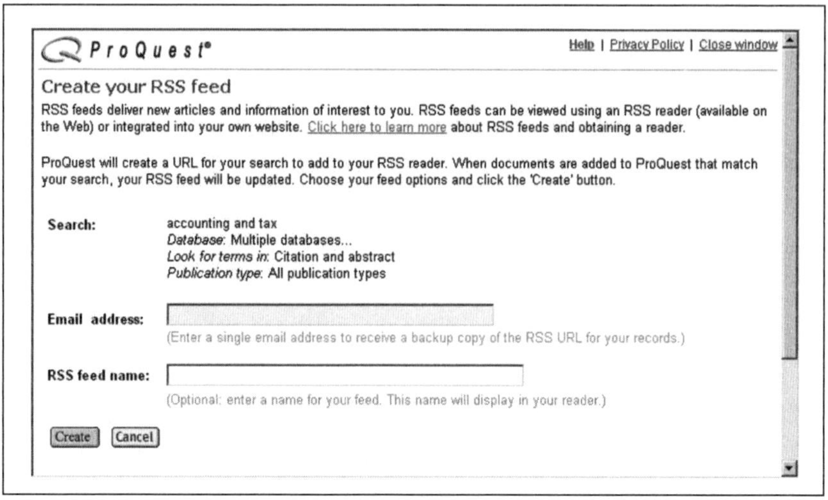

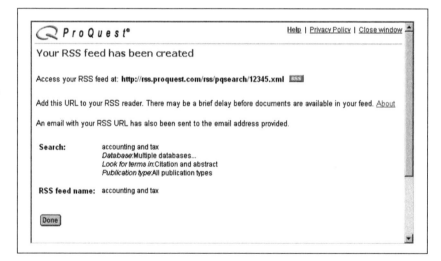

Figure 2.3: Illustration of Setup Page for a Custom RSS Feed

Figure 2.4: Illustration of URL and Confirmation Page for a Custom RSS Feed

search alerts. Citation metadata for matching new content are sent to the RSS application software module for processing. The RSS application module places the citation data into the appropriate XML document, stores it at the appropriate location (URL), and updates the time-date stamp on the page.

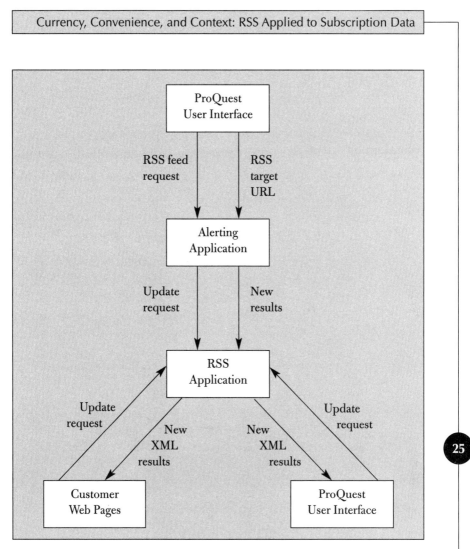

Figure 2.5: System Diagram for ProQuest Custom RSS Feeds

The Integration of RSS Feeds into Web Pages

Here is a simple step-by-step process for adding a ProQuest RSS feed to your Web site using Feed2JS, a utility made available by Maricopa Community Colleges

1. Find an RSS feed that interests you at
   http://www.proquest.com/proquest/rss/rss.shtml
2. Click on the RSS button for the topic of interest to go to the page for that feed. Copy the URL from the address bar.

Sample URL:
http://rss.proquest.com/rss/cmf/abi/Marketing_Advertising.xml

3. Go to
http://jade.mcli.dist.maricopa.edu/feed/index.php?s=build

4. Paste the URL into the URL field and select additional display options (e.g., number of items to show, show/hide descriptions, launch links in new window)

5. Generate the JavaScript code by clicking the button at the bottom of the page. Sample JavaScript code:

```
<script                              language="JavaScript"
src="http://jade.mcli.dist.maricopa.edu/feed/feed2js.php?
src=http%3A%2F%2Frss.proquest.com%2Frss%2Fcmf%
2Fabi%2FMarketing_Advertising.xml&amp;chan=title&
amp;num=5&amp;desc=1"type="text/javascript"></script>
<noscript>
<a
href="http://jade.mcli.dist.maricopa.edu/feed/feed2js.php
?src=http%3A%2F%2Frss.proquest.com%2Frss%2Fcmf%
2Fabi%2FMarketing_Advertising.xml&amp;chan=title&
amp;num= 5&amp;desc=1&amp;html=y">View RSS feed
</a>
</noscript>
```

6. Cut and paste the JavaScript code into your HTML where you want the feed to appear. A sample HTML page is shown in Figure 2.6.

You may of course change the appearance of the feed at the target html page using cascading style sheets.

Value to the Library Mission

A recent study by Outsell, a research and advisory firm, indicates that users are spending more time looking for information. What does this mean for libraries and information providers?

Outsell's "Information Industry User Habits" study compared changes in information usage practices since 2001 by surveying 8,000 users across multiple disciplines. A key finding of the study

ProQuest: Marketing—Advertising

- Guinness and the role of strategic storytelling
  John Simmons.
  Journal of Strategic Marketing.
  London: Mar 2006.
  Vol. 14, Iss. 1;
  p. 11
  [Abstract]
- Seeing the small picture: Ad-self versus ad-culture congruency in international advertising
  Chingching Chang.
  Journal of Business and Psychology.
  New York: Mar 2006.
  Vol. 20, Iss. 3;
  p. 445
  [Abstract]

Figure 2.6: Sample HTML Page Displaying RSS Feed Contents

is that users are spending 30% more time finding information than analyzing it. Outsell suggests that some of the change may be due to disintermediation of the library.

"Open Web search is the most common means for users to access Web content. But increasingly, the limitations of generalized search are becoming known. This is creating opportunities for proactive personalized content delivery, RSS-powered self-aggregation, specialized vertical search, and content integrated into users' most critical applications. Of these, self-aggregation using RSS feeds and vertical search are the trends with the most potential for eating into the growth and share-of-day of generalized search."

— Outsell report on Search, Aggregation, and Distribution Services, October 2005.

In this context, RSS-based applications and services offer librarians the opportunity to both satisfy a growing patron need and reverse the trend toward disintermediation by reinserting libraries into the research process.

Users, RSS Readers, and Self-Aggregation

In the Outsell study referenced above, three-quarters of the survey respondents identified integration of content into their workflow environments as "very important." Major Internet players, recognizing and encouraging this trend, are offering RSS-powered applications.

Mozilla Firefox has an integrated RSS reader. There are indications that Microsoft will integrate RSS capabilities either into Internet Explorer or Windows or both. Google and Yahoo! now incorporate RSS feeds into their popular services. Yahoo's MyWeb2.0 and e-mail application both include the ability to integrate RSS feeds. Google has introduced RSS into their Gmail service and launched Google Lens as an RSS reader late in 2005. According to the Google Lens product manager, work is under way at Google to integrate the two services. These applications will further fuel a significant growth in the use of RSS among the general Web population.

A March 2006 online survey measured interest among ProQuest end users of custom RSS feeds. The pie chart in Figure 2.7 illustrates the relative level of interest among the various different types of users. (Please note that the survey did not provide any definition of RSS or describe what was meant by a custom RSS feed.) High school students indicate a higher level of interest in RSS than undergraduate students. This might reflect that awareness of RSS applications is higher among the high school population. The trend suggests that interest will increase among the college students as today's high school students graduate and move into the university environment.

As users shift from a "search" to a "subscribe and filter" method of managing information, RSS introduces a way to provide alerts to new content that fit a user's predefined set of needs. Thus, self-aggregation using RSS feeds in this way is positioned to take off.

"For all content providers, the data presents confirmation that users are increasingly discerning of the information they consume. . . . In a sense, individuals are themselves becoming

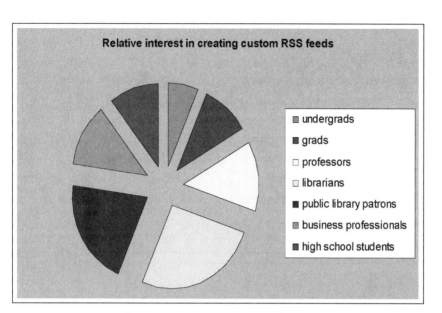

Figure 2.7: Online Survey of ProQuest End Users, March 2006

aggregators—a trend that will no doubt be amplified as RSS enters the mainstream."

— EPS INSIGHTS, May 9, 2005,
http://www.epsltd.com/locate.asp?go=updateNotes

Custom Library Services

RSS is emerging as a more lightweight technology, enabling new types of highly customized current awareness services. When users need access to frequently updated or time-sensitive content, RSS provides an elegantly simple solution.

"Currently there may be a limited amount of content available via RSS in a given subject area, but content available via RSS is rapidly increasing. Increasingly, RSS or RSS-like technologies are also being used in innovative ways . . . offer[ing] a method by which libraries can deeply integrate content from other sites."

— Integrating Information Resources:
Principles, Technologies, and Approaches
Heather Christenson and Roy Tennant, August 15, 2005

Illustrations of library application of RSS feeds for subscription databases follow

- Library Page: Add links containing the latest news and information to your main library page (see Figure 2.8)
- Faculty Page: Instructors can add RSS links to their Web page so students can access additional content relevant to recent and upcoming lectures (see Figure 2.9)
- Course Syllabus: Professors can set up links to articles of interest that are related to designated course assignments (see Figure 2.10)

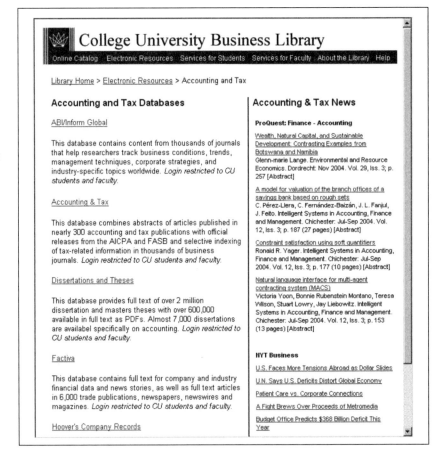

Figure 2.8: Library E-resources Page with RSS Feeds Integration

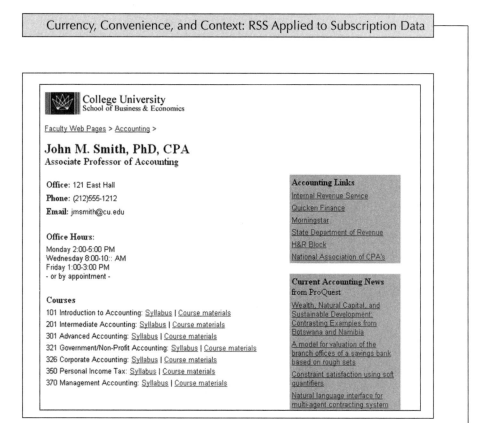

Figure 2.9: Faculty Page with RSS Feeds Integration on the Right

31

The two most prominent applications of RSS feeds from subscription databases might be their integration with library subject guides and with learning management systems. Librarians are rapidly identifying compelling applications for RSS feeds, from providing feeds for delivery announcements of library services information (see RSS feeds for health care from the University of Manitoba Library) to integration of premium content feeds into their library Web sites. Particularly compelling is the ability to display dynamic, topic-specific feeds into their various subject pages. RSS readers initially took root in the library among tech-savvy library staff members, but now using RSS readers is about as commonplace as reading blogs. RSS is even the preferred access point for monitoring blog activity.

Many course management system products support RSS feeds. Faculty instructors, by recognizing the importance of content and

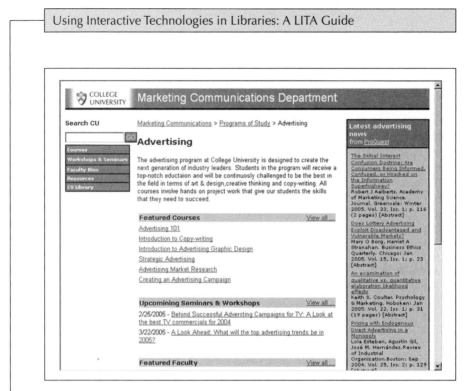

Figure 2.10: College Department Web Page with RSS Feeds Integration on the Right

the power of simple technology, can easily integrate dynamic content into their course sites. As one example, Blackboard supports RSS feeds in their Academic Suite as a connections channel. According to Blackboard staff, this is a popular option among end users.

Potential Issues

As with most technological innovations, there are issues to accompany the opportunities. For RSS feeds from subscription databases, the key issue is authentication. While the feed itself is free to be made available on the open Web, following citation links from the feed to the full text requires authentication to the licensed database.

Since the most common method for authentication is via IP address recognition, authentication of links to full text from RSS feeds are generally only an issue for users offsite. For remote users, existing authentication solutions can be applied.

The most popular approach for remote user authentication at universities and colleges is the application of proxy servers. In this case RSS feeds can incorporate a proxy prefix, pre-pending the proxy server URL to the links to full text in the RSS feed. When the user follows the link, they will be directed through the proxy server—which will require signing in, but only once per session—to the subscription database's full text content.

For public libraries, the remote authentication problem is pervasive even for non-RSS functions, but the same solutions that enable remote access to subscription databases can be applied to authenticate remote users in linking from RSS feed citations to the full text.

Future Uses

As social networks take root in academic research arenas and as licensed content providers introduce the opportunity for users to tag content by adding categories, notes, or references, RSS offers the possibility for researchers to subscribe to colleagues' feeds of tagged content. This practice would facilitate connections between different groups of researchers, accelerate the dissemination of research findings, and build robust online communities through networked information.

33

"Nature Publishing Group's Connotea, built with the del.icio.us technology, is described as "a free online reference management service for scientists." It also recognizes links to certain Websites and automatically collects the bibliographic information for the referenced article or book and enables users to add as many tags as they like, including phrases. Clicking on one of the tag names beneath an article title takes the user to a page that lists all the links given that tag by other users, and provides terms that have been applied to the same content by other users. Every page listing bookmarks on Connotea has a link to an RSS feed."

— EPS Focus Report, "Do you believe in Web 2.0?" February 2006.

Through a combination of simple, easily adaptable technology and user interaction with content, new information assets are created. While this approach to information organization is not distinctly at odds with conventional library science, it marks a significant departure from the conventional practices. Libraries and librarians are pivotal in guiding and shaping these developments to information organizations.

Conclusion

Pragmatic new technologies are catalysts for new user behaviors that often create compelling opportunities in the marketplace. Tracking user behavior is fundamental to ensuring that a product or service continues to meet the target market's needs. RSS is a simple application of a now-commonplace technology (XML). Its simplicity allows for low-cost, rapid adoption by content providers and libraries alike.

"I'm giving a presentation at an upcoming conference on how faculty can use RSS feeds to enrich their WebCT (or BlackBoard, etc.) classes. I just started playing around with your RSS feeds for ABI/Inform—excellent work! I just wanted to send encouragement to expand this availability to all of your databases and to cover a wide range of academic disciplines. Also, is there any chance that you think you'll be offering customizable feeds for keyword searches? I seem to recall that Innovative was working on something along those lines.

Keep up the good work—and keep those feeds coming!"

— Michelle Drumm, Public Services Librarian
Houston Community College System

RSS is fueling a revolution in the use of content, and ProQuest is working to ensure that the benefits extend to licensed content. As an earlier adopter of RSS technology, ProQuest is able to simultaneously encourage and engage new user behaviors that significantly increase the accessibility and value of our research databases.

RSS and RSS-based technologies underlie and enable changes to how users perform research and manage information consumption.

Application of RSS to licensed databases is a natural and necessary progression. This trend and the simple technologies fueling it present a multitude of opportunities for the library community to extend and redefine services for patrons.

"The result is less reliance on search and more on "human filtering and alerting" to find information of value."

— Outsell report on Search, Aggregation,
and Distribution Services, October 2005.

New models for leveraging the phenomenal new online reach and engagement opportunities involving RSS are rapidly evolving. Libraries can become a more integral part of the mix by taking advantage of user shifts to new tools and consumption patterns.

References

Christenson, Heather, and Roy Tennant. 2005. "Integrating Information Resources: Principles, Technologies, and Approaches." http://www.cdlib.org/inside/projects/metasearch/nsdl/nsdl_report2.pdf.

EPS. 2005. "EPS Insights." http://www.epsltd.com/locate.asp?go=update Notes.

Outsell. 2005. "Information Industry User Habits." outsellinc.com.

Worlock, Kate and Majied Robinson. EPS. 2006. "EPS Focus Report, 'Do You Believe in Web 2.0?'." epsltd.com/clients/viewBriefing Report.asp

35

Notes

Notes

Chapter 3

Wiki as Research Guide

Chad F. Boeninger

Abstract

Many libraries and librarians use Web-based subject guides or pathfinders to direct researchers to reference books, online databases, and Web sites. These guides usually consist of static html pages that may or may not be regularly edited or updated. Wiki software can be used in conjunction with research guide content to deliver dynamic information to library patrons. A Wiki can help a librarian easily create and maintain up-to-date and relevant information in order to better serve the research community.

39

About the Author

Chad F. Boeninger is a reference and instruction librarian at Ohio University's Alden Library. He is also the business and economics bibliographer and assistant Web manager. Chad began working at Ohio University in July 2002, shortly after receiving his Master of Information Sciences from the University of Tennessee. Chad's research interests include multiple aspects of technology, library marketing, library planning, library instruction, and public services. He is constantly striving to make the library an enjoyable place and a viable resource for current and future patrons. He is the author of the Library Voice blog.

Introduction

One of the challenges that libraries and librarians face is how to educate patrons and users about finding and using quality information.

With the growth of the Internet, this challenge is even more pronounced, as many patrons think Google has the answer to everything. Librarians know that there is a plethora of information that is not freely available on the Web, and they purchase many different formats of resources so that their users will have access to quality information resources. Libraries purchase these resources so that patrons will have the resources they need to conduct research, seek new knowledge, or make informed decisions. However, because some patrons believe that Google does hold all the answers, it becomes increasingly difficult to get library patrons to use these valuable and expensive library resources. It also becomes increasingly important to acknowledge the utility of resources in which the library invests.

Many public and academic libraries and librarians try to address this issue by offering library instruction sessions to the research community. In these sessions, librarians generally teach basic search skills while pointing the researchers to specific resources that will address the specific information need. These instruction sessions are also done on a much smaller scale during reference transactions between an individual and a librarian. Unfortunately, these educational opportunities are only effective for the researcher who attends a class or consults the reference desk, and both require either that the patron visit the physical library or take the initiative to contact the library, or for librarians to be proactive in contacting faculty or students in their subject areas.

Fortunately, the Internet gives librarians the ability to make their resources available to patrons who do not come to the library. One way librarians promote resources and research skills is through Web-based subject guides. Generally, these subject guides (also called pathfinders or research guides) give listings of useful resources in a particular subject area. If subject guides are placed at intuitive locations on a library Web site, and if they contain up-to-date content, then they can be very useful resources for recommending resources for patrons. Most subject guides are static html Web pages that require someone with Web-authoring skills and/or specialized Web-authoring software to create and maintain the pages. Because of these restrictions, the static pages may only be edited by one person (such as the library Webmaster) or at one location (such as the office machine that has Dreamweaver installed). These limitations may hinder timely edits of static Web pages, so the content of the research guide may not be as up-to-date as the librarian would like.

A Wiki can help a librarian or library in this matter, by allowing the librarian to have a dynamic Web presence that is easy to update, is user-friendly, and promotes community. A Wiki, which in its simplest definition is a Web page that can be edited by anyone via an intuitive Web-based interface, can enable a librarian to create and maintain up-to-date research content for the patron community. I have been using a Wiki to promote resources and research skills to business researchers at Ohio University. My experiences, successes, and lessons learned are chronicled here.

The Need for Change

At Ohio University Libraries, each professional librarian serves as a subject bibliographer for one or more academic departments or colleges. As the subject bibliographer for the College of Business, I am fortunate to serve 1,700 students and over 70 faculty members from the college. I am also very fortunate to have opportunities to deliver library instruction sessions to approximately 300–500 students each quarter. Between the number of instruction opportunities that I have and the overall difficulty of doing business research, I have a great deal of contact with faculty and student researchers. As I am the only librarian on staff who specializes in the area of business, it can sometimes be a little overwhelming during the busier times in the quarter.

The business curriculum consists largely of project-based group work. For example, the sophomore business cluster class generally has about 40 students. The students are divided into eight groups of five, and each group has the same or a similar project. For example, each group might each be assigned to demonstrate

41

why their individual company is the best company to work for in America, or each group might have to develop a business plan for a local company. Each quarter, there are two sophomore business cluster groups (80 students total), two junior business cluster groups (another 80 students), the MBA cohort (50 students), nine Professional Communication classes (about 250 students), and other individual business and marketing classes.

Each quarter presents new challenges as I get to learn about different companies, industries, resources, and business terms as I help the students learn how to find the information they need. While I do have the opportunity to talk to students in a number of the classes, I do not get to talk to all of them. Even with some of students that I do talk to, I only usually get an hour with them and thus cannot possibly address all of the current and future questions. There are always follow-up questions when the students really start researching their projects, and the students can contact me in person or via IM, e-mail, or phone. However, I am not always available when they need an answer, so they must use other resources or my colleagues in my absence.

42

A library research guide is one mechanism that librarians can create to empower researchers to find appropriate resources. Because of the abundance of business databases and reference tools, I had three different research guides—one for general business, one for international business, and one for marketing. Like many librarians, I hoped that researchers would use these guides to help them in their research. These guides were static html pages that listed the best resources for doing business research, and the guides were prominently linked from numerous places on our library Web site. I had three different guides because I originally thought that separating the guides by broad topic would make them easier to use. Each guide was organized by broad research categories (such as company information, industry information, and general information) to facilitate finding information.

While trying my best to make these guides user-friendly, I became increasingly dissatisfied with how difficult they could be to use. For example, a user might have to look in all three guides in order to find what he/she was looking for. There were some resources that were listed only in one of the research guides, while there were other resources that were listed in all three guides. This redundancy of resources was potentially confusing to the users, and they also made the guides more difficult to update. If I needed to change something about a particular resource, I often had to make changes to three separate html files. Another frustrating element concerning the three research guides was the lack of a search function. Users could use the "find" feature of their Web browsers, but this only searched the text of one html page, not all three at once. Once again, a user would have to go to all three guides to perform the same text search to find information.

Having three research guides made updates difficult, so I usually only updated the guides once a year. Eventually, I have come to use the research guides rarely myself and only updated them because I thought that, as a bibliographer, I was supposed to create and maintain library research guides. With out-of-date content in guides that I did not even use myself, how could I expect business students and faculty to use the guides? There had to be a better way to create, edit, and communicate relevant library resources to the user community.

Setting Up the Wiki

In July 2005, I did find a better way, when I began using a Wiki as a research guide. Wikis are generally database-driven Web sites that can be easily edited through a Web interface. With a Wiki, a user can create dynamic content easily and quickly without the need for Web-authoring software or html editing skills. Wikis are often edited by a community of users which can promote community and collaboration. Probably the best known Wiki is Wikipedia. While the reliability of the content of Wikipedia is under constant scrutiny, the overall organization and findability of information receive much less criticism. After using Wikipedia and

43

other Wikis to find information, I began to see how a Wiki might be used to replace my research guides.

To start, I downloaded and installed MediaWiki on our Web server. I would love to say that I evaluated a number of different software options, but basically I chose MediaWiki because it is the same software that Wikipedia uses. Because it is used by Wikipedia, I figured that the MediaWiki developers would continue to release new updates for the software. I also reasoned that I could use Wikipedia as a guide in organizing and formatting my Wiki. Finally, having a Wiki that is very similar to Wikipedia can make the use of the Wiki much more simple, as some users will already be familiar with the Wiki's functions and structure.

MediaWiki is open source software that can be downloaded for free at www.mediawiki.org, so the only costs in setting up and maintaining a Wiki are the space on the Web server and the labor in the installation and maintenance. MediaWiki requires PHP and MySQL in order to run, so the initial installation process may need to be performed by someone with Web server administration experience. Installing software on a Web server may not be a realistic option for some, but there are other alternatives. Wiki hosting services are available for free or for a monthly charge and offer easy setup. PbWiki is one such service and claims that setting up a Wiki is as easy as making a peanut butter sandwich. While hosting services such as pbWiki do offer ease of installation, it should be noted that most do not offer the customization options that a locally hosted Wiki will. With a MediaWiki—or other locally-hosted Wiki installations—there are more opportunities for customization of the Wiki than with Wikis that are hosted through Wiki-hosting services. With a Wiki that is installed on a library's own server, the library will have the ability to customize or change nearly any setting or file in the Wiki installation.

After setting up the Wiki, I began populating the Wiki with some of the key resources from my three business research guides. This allowed me to keep the most useful content while discarding the lists of less useful resources. Determining which resources to add first was rather easy, as I simply wrote Wiki pages for the resources that I used and recommended the most. There were many resources in the old html research guides that I did not use that often, so I either decided not to include them in the Wiki or deferred them to the bottom of the to-be-added list. While cutting and pasting from the research guides to the Wiki, I also added more content for each particular resource. In doing so, I hoped to add value to the resources by demonstrating how the resources could be used to satisfy a particular research need. My old research guides gave the title, location and call number, and a brief description of the resource. In contrast, the pages for each resource on the Wiki include the title, location and call number, a more in-depth description of the resource, and key ways to use the resource.

The Biz Wiki's Content

After a few weeks of adding some content and organization to the Wiki, and after customizing the look and feel of the Wiki, I released the Biz Wiki for its debut in July of 2005. As described on the main page, "the Biz Wiki is a collection of business information resources available through Ohio University Libraries. It is designed to assist business researchers in finding the best resources for their projects or topics. The Biz Wiki contains articles about business reference books, databases, Web sites, and other research guides. Nearly all of the resources will only be available to current members of the Ohio University community, as many of the resources are subscription databases or local reference resources."

The Biz Wiki contains two different types of articles. One type may be referred to as reference content. Each reference content article is essentially an article about one reference tool. For example, the Biz Wiki article for *Demographics USA, County Edition* in Figure 3.1 contains the call number and location of this key reference book, as well as the type of information that the user may find in the resource. The information in a Wiki article is generally a great deal more in depth than the user would find in the library catalog record.

45

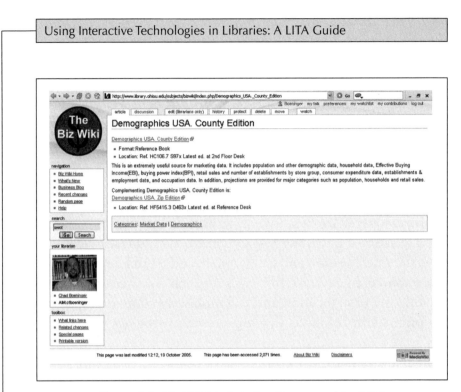

Figure 3.1: Biz Wiki Article for Demographics USA

The second type of article may be referred to as instructional content. These articles generally list several resources that a researcher may wish to consult for a topic. One example of this type of article is the Biz Wiki article on finding a SWOT analysis. This article explains that a SWOT analysis is an examination or a company's strengths, weaknesses, opportunities, and threats, and it points the researcher to appropriate resources. In the SWOT analysis article (Figure 3.2), I explain that many analyses may be found in a particular database, but I also attempt to demonstrate the importance of looking at additional resources (which are also listed).

Other examples of instructional content include the company research basics and industry research basics articles. These articles are two of the most popular pages in the Biz Wiki. The articles walk the researcher through the process of basic business research while pointing the researcher to appropriate resources. These articles discuss various types of business information and how the size, location, or type of company or industry can influence how

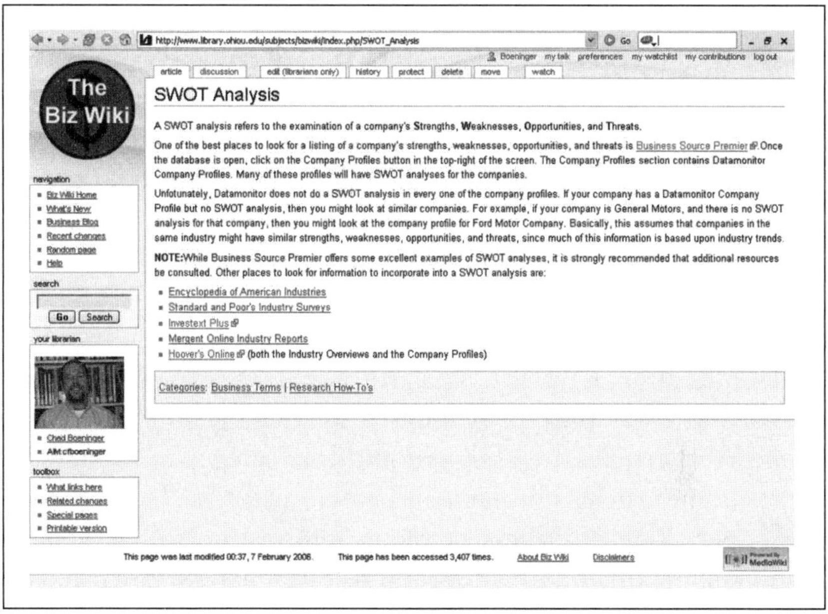

Figure 3.2: Biz Wiki Article for SWOT Analysis

much information is available. I also have tried to embed "nuggets" of information literacy concepts into many of the instructional content articles. As an example, I have written about the importance of understanding author bias when reading a company's annual report.

The Biz Wiki's Organization and Search Features

Upon arriving on the Biz Wiki's main page, a researcher may either browse the content by category or search by keyword. The search interface is effective, albeit rudimentary. The search function is very simple, allowing the user to type in a string of words with no Boolean connectors necessary. For example, a search of "company report annual" will retrieve the same exact results as "company and annual and report." This is because the word "and" is a stopword in MySQL (the database that runs the Wiki) and is not counted. Usually the stopwords do not pose a problem, with the exception of attempting to search for "SIC" (for Standard Industrial

Classification). MySQL ignores "SIC" as a stopword, so searching for those letters retrieves no results. These few problems aside, the ability to search the Biz Wiki is a very powerful and useful feature. I have had several of my fellow reference librarians tell me that all they had to do was search for "swot" in the Wiki to find information for patrons doing SWOT analyses. If my colleagues find the search function useful, odds are that the student researchers are using it as well.

Users of the Biz Wiki may also browse the Wiki's categories to find information. Each Biz Wiki article is assigned a specific category according to the type of information that the article contains. Some Wiki articles are assigned multiple categories to increase access to the article. The main, or parent, categories (general business, international business, company information, industry information, marketing information, and research how-to) are listed on the front page of the Wiki. Users can click on a category to find articles within that category or to find more specific subcategories within the category. The categories also work well if a researcher finds an article after using the search feature of the Wiki. If the article that the researcher finds is useful, then he or she may also look at similar articles by clicking on the article's category link at the bottom of the page. To a certain extent, this organization scheme works similarly to the keyword to subject-heading search skills that librarians teach in library instruction sessions. Figure 3.3 contains a list of some of the Biz Wiki's categories.

Another Wiki feature that facilitates the finding of information is the ability to interlink or cross-reference articles. As an example, if a researcher searches for "Industry Ratios" by using the search function, he or she may find the article for *Industry Norms and Key Business Ratios*, a key reference source for finding financial ratios for specific industries. This article discusses the content of the book and it also cross-references or links to the *Industry Financial Ratios* article, which discusses other resources (such as Mergent Online, Hoover's Online, and Research Insight) that can be used to find the information. Likewise, the company research

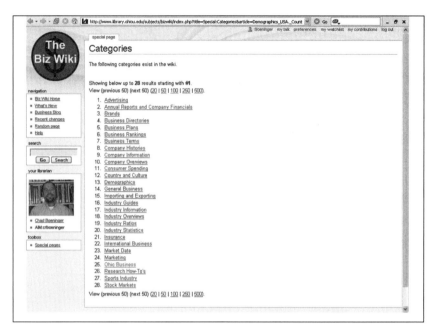

Figure 3.3: Categories in the Biz Wiki

basics page links to the industry research basics article, as business researchers will at times need both types of information for their projects.

49

Adding and Editing Content

Keeping the content current or adding new articles is incredibly easy with the Biz Wiki. Since all edits and additions of content are done via a Web interface (see Figure 3.4), content can be created easily and quickly, without the need for specialized html-editing software. Wiki software uses a type of Wiki language, but generally the Wiki language is very simple and easy to learn. Many Wiki programs have a built-in editor, allowing the user to perform simple formatting functions with a click of a mouse. With the Web-based interface, I have added and updated Wiki content at my desk, at the reference desk, in the classroom, and even from home.

Because the Wiki is so easy to update, it is very easy to generate new content that really meets the needs of the research community.

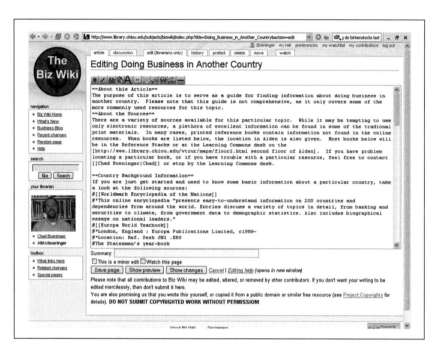

Figure 3.4: The Web-based Interface

I have found that with each new project that the business students work on, I discover new resources and different research methods that can help them with their projects. In other words, as the students are learning about their company or industry, their questions give me ample opportunity to continue learning as well. Questions they have about business research help drive the content of the Biz Wiki. Whether the question comes in the form by e-mail, IM, or personal conversation, the odds are good that if one student is asking the question, there are plenty of others with the same question.

As an example, I received a reference e-mail from a student asking about sources for importing and exporting regulations. I replied to the student with the answer and sent him some links to several resources in the Biz Wiki. The same day, I received the same reference question from two other students via e-mail and instant messaging. During the instant messaging conversation, I

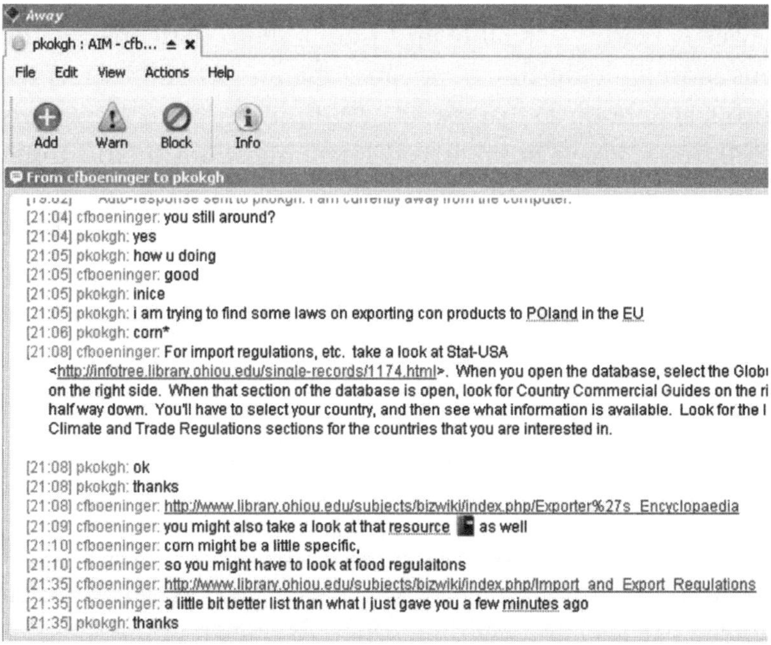

Figure 3.5: Creating Wiki Content during a Reference Transaction

took the content of the response to the original message and created a new Biz Wiki article. This is shown in Figure 3.5. In the conversation below, there is a fifteen-minute gap between 21:10 and 21:35. This is because during that time I was putting together the content of the import and export regulations Wiki article. At 21:35, I sent the patron the link to the Wiki article.

When I put several tips to finding import and export regulations on the Wiki, I got the information out of my e-mail and onto the open Web. As a result, anyone with the same questions can now have access to the answer. By putting the answer in the Biz Wiki, research help for this question is available at times when I might not be. Putting the information on the Biz Wiki makes my job easier as well. Whenever I get a similar question via IM or e-mail, I no longer have to type out a long response or search my mailbox for the answer. I simply have to look for the article in the Biz Wiki and send the patron the link to the article. The answer is readily available and I am able to help answer questions more quickly. Since I created the import and export regulations article on February 14, 2006, it has been viewed over 1,800 times. I have not received 1,800 questions on this topic in the past six months, so apparently others find the information they need without necessarily contacting me directly. This use shows that by identifying and addressing common questions, a librarian can create content that will be useful to current and future researchers.

Measuring Usage of the Biz Wiki

Measuring usage is one of the most powerful features of using a Wiki as a research guide. The MediaWiki software measures each time an individual Wiki article is accessed. The software also displays a list of popular pages (see Figure 3.6) that sorts the most popular articles in descending order. As shown in the screenshot below, I can see that the industry research basics and company research basics guides are very heavily used, considering that those two articles were only created three months ago.

It is very satisfying to see that the main page of the Biz Wiki has been accessed over 31,000 times since it was created. When compared to other electronic resources, the Biz Wiki has been one of the most popular resources each quarter. I believe one reason for this is that it makes information readily available and easy to find. I have also tried to do as much as I can to promote the Wiki to students, faculty, and library colleagues. I have placed links to the Biz Wiki in prominent places on the library Web site. I promote the Wiki when I speak to business classes. Finally, I have even used some of the pages in the Biz Wiki as an outline during library instruction sessions.

Challenges

In a perfect world, I would not be the only one promoting the Biz Wiki and creating its content. When I initially built the Biz Wiki, I

Figure 3.6: Popular Pages in the Biz Wiki

had hoped that students, faculty, and other library colleagues would appreciate the opportunity to add their own content and ideas to the Wiki. Community contributions and editing is really the strength behind most Wikis, and that collaboration has the potential to build both an excellent resource and a strong user community. Unfortunately, I have yet to have any faculty, students, or library colleagues add content to the Biz Wiki. When I built the Biz Wiki, I set it up so that anyone could edit the content. The Wiki began to get flooded with spam, so I disabled anonymous edits and required users to register before making changes to the Wiki. Unfortunately, spammers were still persistent and went the extra step to create accounts in order to post links to their very inappropriate Web sites. As a last resort, I locked the Biz Wiki down so that only I can create user accounts. I placed a message on the login screen and in various places on the Wiki, inviting users to contact me if they would like an account. Thus far, no one has taken me up on the offer. While this is far from ideal if I wish to encourage community editing, this was a measure that I had to take to control Wiki spam.

The lack of community editing was discouraging at first, but it no longer bothers me. Even though the research community is not using the Biz Wiki in every way that I had originally intended, the numbers speak for themselves and tell me that the Biz Wiki is being used. The number of hits provides feedback that the Biz Wiki is a useful resource, and comments from students, faculty, and librarians also confirm the strength of the resource. One of my colleagues recently told me: "I had some students who were looking for a SWOT analysis, but you weren't around. I searched for 'swot' in the Biz Wiki, and we found what they were looking for." I really appreciate comments like that because they reassure me that the Biz Wiki is working as planned.

Conclusion

Using a Wiki as a research guide has made me more efficient in delivering library information by allowing me to make information available to researchers wherever and whenever they need it. I have been very pleased with my experience of using a Wiki as a research guide and I have no intentions of returning to my old traditional html guides. Only time will tell how the Biz Wiki will be used in the future, but I will continue to add and edit content on an ongoing basis, while weeding pages that are no longer relevant or out-of-date. It is my hope that the Wiki will continue to be a viable and useful resource to business researchers at my institution and beyond. If the day should come when the Biz Wiki is no longer useful, I am sure there will be another new technology that will also facilitate delivery of information to library patrons.

References and Further Reading

Boeninger, Chad. 2005. "A Wiki as a Research Guide." Library Voice Blog. http://libraryvoice.com/archives/2005/07/13/a-wiki-as-a-research-guide/

Farkas, Meredith. 2005. "So You Want to Build a Wiki." WebJunction. http://Webjunction.org/do/DisplayContent?id=11262 (accessed September 4, 2006).

Farkas, Meredith. 2006. "Wiki World." http://libsuccess.org/index.php?title=Wiki_World, (accessed September 4, 2006).

Stephens, Michael. 2006. *Web 2.0 and Libraries: Best Practices for Social Software*. Chicago, IL: ALA TechSource.

Notes

Notes

Chapter 4

Library Blogs:
The New Technology
Bandwagon

Steven J. Bell

Abstract

As new technologies become available, there is often both external
and internal pressure in the library profession to "jump on the
bandwagon" and quickly start using the new technology. Implementing a technology without determining whether the library
community really needs it or how it will benefit them, whether it is
done to stay ahead of the crowd, for prestige, or simply to keep up
with technology fads, is at best a questionable allocation of the library's resources. This chapter uses the library blog as a case
study to illustrate some of the pitfalls and promises of new technologies. This case study describes how an academic library,
rather than just establishing a blog in the hope that someone
would read it, used technology to "push" the blog postings into
student's courseware sites. As a result, readership of the blog in-
creased, and students found the postings useful.

About the Author

Steven J. Bell is director of the Paul J. Gutman Library at Philadelphia
University. Prior to that he was assistant director at the Wharton
School at the University of Pennsylvania, where he also earned his
Ed.D. in 1997. He writes and speaks frequently on topics such as

59

information retrieval, library and learning technologies, and academic librarianship. An adjunct professor at the Drexel University College of Information Science and Technology, he teaches courses in online searching, academic librarianship, and business information resources. He maintains a Web site, Steven Bell's Keeping Up Web Site, and Weblog, The Kept-Up Academic Librarian, which promote current awareness skills and resources. Steven is a co-founder of the Blended Librarian's Online Learning Community on the Learning Times Network and has participated in numerous virtual presentations. For additional information about the author or to find links to the various Web sites he publishes and maintains, go to http://staff.philau.edu/bells.

Introduction

Think back a few years ago to the dawn of the virtual reference era. At first, a few libraries experimented with call center software or even plain old instant messenger clients. Librarians of that era will recall the anticipation of this new technology. The possibility of tapping into younger patrons' enthusiasm for chat communication was a source of excitement for the virtual reference pioneers. One of librarians' great strengths is our enthusiasm for spotting new technologies and ability to rapidly deploy them in delivering services to our user communities. One of librarians' real weaknesses is our enthusiasm for finding and implementing new technologies before we really know if they make sense for both us and our user communities. In re-examining the virtual reference frenzy, there are obvious parallels between it and what has developed into an infatuation with library blogs and the hope of what they might deliver.

In many libraries that adopted virtual reference, it became clear that the library's enthusiasm for the technology was unmatched within user communities. Many of these services were little used and eventually languished (Coffman and Arret, 2004). Just because library users utilized the technology did not mean they wanted to chat with us. For many librarians, the perceived disappointments of the virtual reference movement became concrete when Steve Coffman, one of virtual reference's earliest advocates, published an article that elaborated on various failures of virtual reference (Coffman and Arret, 2004). Many libraries came to realize that the effort virtual reference involved, such as training and scheduling issues, was not worth the few chats a month. Some libraries decided that only a simple instant messenger client was worth the effort. Others found some value in virtual reference by joining larger networks.

The entire experience suggests that the library community should have asked more fundamental questions about virtual reference: Is this something the user community wants or cares about? Where does offering any new technology-based service fit into the library's list of service priorities? Those libraries that have discovered the path to success with virtual reference are those that thoughtfully considered such concerns and implemented the technology in a sensible way that meets their own and their community's best interests.

Success or failure in implementation of new technologies can depend on how thoughtfully the process is approached. Library blogs offer both promise and pitfalls. With so many crucial challenges confronting our libraries in these uncertain times, are we truly gaining the greatest return on investment from the time put into developing and maintaining the latest and untested technologies? Or, as Walt Crawford, the renowned onetime *American Libraries* columnist and author of the online publication *Cites & Insights* (http://citesandinsights.info/), might put it, are we just exercising our fixation with a shiny new toy?

Are we engaging with this new technology because we are certain it can help us to achieve our established outcomes for user access to and use of information, or is this simply another case of technology infatuation? Libraries will be increasingly challenged to find the right balance between experimenting with new and potentially productive technologies and avoiding the temptation to jump onto the latest technology bandwagon because some

pundit claims it is the next must-have ("killer app") for techno-
logically savvy libraries. Library professionals must learn to improve their decision-making process when it comes to deciding if
and when it is appropriate to integrate new technology into our
array of library services and resources.

Do Your Users Want A Library Blog? Can They Use It?

Some libraries have already jumped on the library blog bandwagon while others are just giving it some thought. A library blog
has real potential for promoting the library to its user community by delivering news and creating awareness about services
and resources. While there may be other uses for library blogs
(a few institutions have experimented with using them for sharing reference information), the vast majority of libraries use their
blog to deliver news and information. Creating a library blog,
however, is the easy part. The hard part is getting the user community to subscribe to and read the blog. Each library contemplating a blog should consider if, realistically, its user community
will want to read the library blog; not just the few who compre-
hend blogging and related technologies such as RSS (real simple
syndication) and news aggregators, but a large enough segment
to make the time and energy that goes into creating the library
blog worthwhile. Considering that our users have millions of
blogs to choose from, what will compel them to read the library
blog regularly?

When I first began to learn about library blogs two years ago,
I was skeptical. There were many questions about their value as a
mechanism for communicating with library patrons. This was not
a case of writing off blogging as a waste of time, nor was it about
being unfamiliar with blogging technology. I read a variety of
blogs, experimented with RSS and different aggregators for years,
and since January 2004 I have maintained my own blog, The
Kept-Up Academic Librarian, at http://keptup.typepad.com.
I heartily endorsed blogging as a tool for communicating with

colleagues, and as an educational technology that was increasingly being used by faculty to promote student writing.

But the issue goes beyond answering the question, "Do the members of the library's user community, be they students, neighbors, faculty, or teens, want or need a library blog?" For most librarians contemplating library blogging, perhaps an even more fundamental and essential question is "Can members of the user community even take advantage of a library blog?" Many individuals may have heard of blogs, but how many are aware of RSS and news aggregator technology? Studies by both Forrester Research and Nielsen Associates in 2005 indicated that less than 10% of computer users knew of or used these technologies, and it must surely have been even less than that at the dawn of library blogs (Best, 2005; Bausch, 2005). More recently OCLC, in its *College Students' Perceptions of Library and Information Resources* study, asked respondents to indicate which technology they had used at least once. From a list of over a dozen technologies, RSS ranked dead last with not even 2% of respondents having ever used it (De Rosa, 2006). Does that bode well for libraries that anticipate their users taking advantage of their blog's RSS feed? If individuals do not use nor have any knowledge of news aggregator, then it is far less likely that they would be able to follow a library blog with any regularity. Blogs without news aggregators are like Web sites without browsers. One is just not practical without the other.

To learn more about my own student community's knowledge of blogging technology, I conducted a brief survey during our fall 2004 semester (the survey is posted at http://intercom.virginia.edu/SurveySuite/Surveys/studenttech/index2.html). Over a two-week period, 252 students had responded. Only 1.9% of the respondents answered "yes" to the question, "Do you know what RSS is or do you currently subscribe to RSS feeds for acquiring news and information?" Less than 1% answered "yes" to the question "Do you subscribe to a news aggregator or do you currently have news aggregator software loaded on your computer?" Seventy-nine percent indicated they had never heard of a news aggregator. The survey confirmed that even my user community, students who are relatively technology savvy, knew little about RSS or news aggregators.

A Better Way to Blog to Your Community

In the autumn of 2004, I began experimenting with a blog for the Paul J. Gutman Library at Philadelphia University. Some healthy skepticism seemed warranted. Since the survey indicated virtually no knowledge of RSS or use of aggregators among the local user community, it boded poorly for launching a library blog. Starting one just because it is possible or because many others already did was an unacceptable rationale. Libraries could always offer workshops on how to use RSS and news aggregators, and use them as opportunities to subscribe attendees to the library blog. But do the librarians have sufficient staff to create and deliver additional workshops, and is it rational to educate users about something they have expressed no interest in learning?

So what can librarians do to increase the odds that the library blog will reach the intended audience? As I tried to figure out what to do with the fledgling library blog, I discovered a technology that eliminated the need to address any of these questions. I discovered that the solution was to push the library blog content to where the users are found so they will see the library blog postings even if they know nothing about RSS or news aggregators. Academic librarians in particular have a great opportunity to do so because they can push library blog content to their institutional courseware. Courseware systems such as Blackboard, WebCT, Angel, and Moodle are becoming ubiquitous in higher education. As with library resources, it makes sense to put the content where the students are, and these days they are busy learning in courseware sites.

RSS to Javascript Converters

During that same fall 2004 semester in which I started a library blog at Gutman Library, I came across a message posted to the

Blackboard Instructional Designers discussion list (its archive is found at http://www.wpunj.edu/irt/list/bb-id/) that described a technology for directing RSS feeds to HTML pages. It was referred to as the RSS-to-Javascript Converter. The converter itself is simply a Web site that, when provided with information about an RSS feed and how it should be displayed on an HTML page, generates several lines of Javascript. That scripting, when cut and pasted into an HTML page, activates the conversion process. The end result is that the RSS feed is directed to a specified HTML page. That means a library blog's postings can be automatically displayed on the announcement page of any course site. For public and other libraries that do not use courseware, this same technology can push blog postings to the library home page, a community home page, or any HTML page.

Using the converter is fairly easy. The following example will explain how it works and will show how the library blog postings display on the courseware announcements page. A preferred converter, for its ease and options, is Feed2JS found at http://feed2js.org/. Begin by entering an RSS feed's URL into the designated spot on the converter. In Figure 4.1, the URL of the RSS feed for "Get It At Gutman," http://gutmanlibrary.typepad.com/

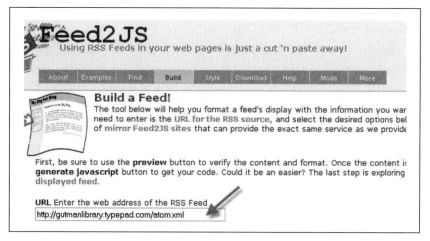

Figure 4.1: Entering the URL of the RSS Feed

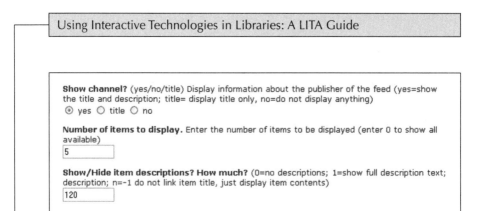

Show channel? (yes/no/title) Display information about the publisher of the feed (yes=show the title and description; title= display title only, no=do not display anything)
⊙ yes ○ title ○ no

Number of items to display. Enter the number of items to be displayed (enter 0 to show all available)
`5`

Show/Hide item descriptions? How much? (0=no descriptions; 1=show full description text; description; n=-1 do not link item title, just display item contents)
`120`

Figure 4.2: Options from the Feed2JS Converter

atom.xml, is shown being entered into the URL box in the Feed2JS interface.

Then, a few options are provided to complete the process. For example, when "show channel" is turned on, it displays the name of the blog and the author. More important is the number of items to display. Left unspecified, every post would be displayed. Given the limited real estate of a courseware announcements page, only a few postings should be displayed, and this is where that number is specified. Several of these options from the Feed2JS converter are shown in Figure 4.2. All of the options, as well as more detailed instructions on using RSS-to-Javascript Converters for this purpose, are described in Low Threshold Application # 44, "Integrating RSS feeds into your course management system" (Wiemer, 2005).

When all of the appropriate option boxes are completed, the request to create the necessary Javascript code is submitted to Feed2JS. It will return a page with the box shown in Figure 4.3.

The next step in the process of integrating the RSS feed into the courseware site is to cut-and-paste the Javascript code into the appropriate space on the course site as shown in Figure 4.4. This is why it is important for academic librarians to gain familiarity with their institutional courseware. Those with a good knowledge of courseware functions will find this operation fairly straightforward and can work effectively with faculty to complete the process.

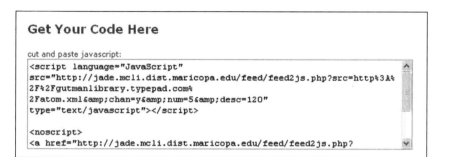

Get Your Code Here

cut and paste javascript:

```
<script language="JavaScript"
src="http://jade.mcli.dist.maricopa.edu/feed/feed2js.php?src=http%3A%
2F%2Fgutmanlibrary.typepad.com%
2Fatom.xml&amp;chan=y&amp;num=5&amp;desc=120"
type="text/javascript"></script>

<noscript>
<a href="http://jade.mcli.dist.maricopa.edu/feed/feed2js.php?
```

Figure 4.3: The Javascript Code

Figure 4.4: The Pasted Javascript Code

When finished, the library blog postings will appear on the designated courseware site's announcements page as shown in Figure 4.5.

If necessary, adjustments can be made by returning to the converter, modifying the options, and generating new Javascript code. From this point forward, whenever a posting is added to the library blog it will automatically appear on the announcements page or other designated HTML page. A public or special library could use this technology to generate the blog postings to

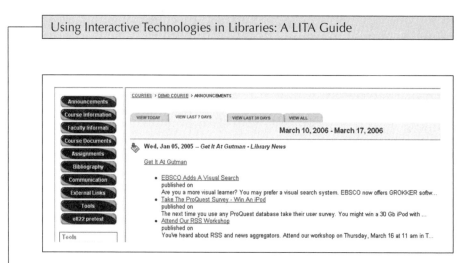

Figure 4.5: The Finished Announcements Page

the library's home page or another page within the library or organization's Web site. An example of this application, as shown if Figure 4.6, can be found on the home page of the library at Philadelphia University (http://gutman.info) where this technology is used to support a library news function.

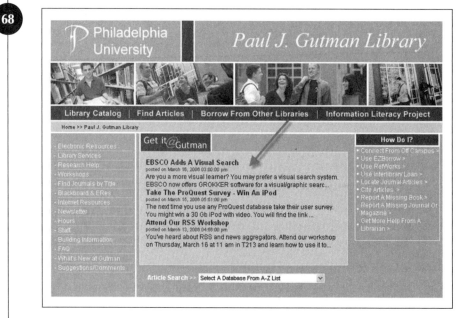

Figure 4.6: Paul J. Gutman Library Home Page Showing Blog

A Student Experiment

With a new understanding of how to "blog to courseware," I decided to experiment with the technology in our spring 2005 semester. Though I possessed the technical ability to feed blog postings to course sites, the critical question "Do the students want, need, or care about library blog postings?" was largely unanswered. Despite the proliferation of library blogs, no concrete evidence exists to support the notion that our users want or need them. After all, they may prefer receiving library news by e-mail. It was important to attempt to learn more about students' use of and reaction to receiving library postings in their courseware. In order to accomplish this, obtaining faculty support for the idea was essential. The course site is the faculty member's domain, and each member's permission is needed to allow a librarian to add the Javascript code. This is yet another reason why it is important for academic librarians to understand how their courseware works and to establish good collaborative relationships with faculty members. Both are necessary for the integration of library resources and services into courseware.

An experiment was initiated in 20 courses. The institutional Blackboard system's internal e-mail function was used to issue a message seeking faculty partners for this experiment. Nearly 40 faculty members responded in the affirmative, allowing me to select 20 courses that represented a good cross section of students and majors. When pasting the code into the announcements page of each course, librarians should be sure to make the announcement permanent so the postings feed to the course beyond seven days. Keep the number of words used to describe each posting to a minimum (100 words or less). These steps will keep the library's blog postings from turning into a Web page real estate hog. All of the courses received the same content as it was fed from the library's sole blog. If the library wanted to target certain categories of news to certain areas of the curriculum (e.g., business news for business courses), it would need a separate blog source directed to that particular area. Owing to positive feedback from faculty and

69

their students, the library blog's feed was integrated into courseware sites again in the 2005–2006 academic year, with the number of courses participating increasing to 50 during the spring 2006 semester.

Reactions to Blogging to Courseware

During the spring semester of 2005 and throughout the 2006 academic year, postings were added to Get It At Gutman, the Gutman Library Weblog, on a regular basis. At the end of each spring semester, I surveyed students in the experimental courses to learn more about how they responded to the library postings. A twelve-question survey was distributed electronically via the Blackboard system, with 97 students responding in 2005 and 72 students responding in 2006. The survey questions and data from 2006 are reported at the end of this chapter. For those wishing to replicate the survey, it can be found at http://intercom.virginia. edu/SurveySuite/Surveys/rssfeedsurvey/index2.html.

What did the survey show? First, the large majority of students (75% in 2005 and 56% in 2006) found the library posts useful and indicated the library should continue to provide this content to the course sites. A much smaller number, 15% in 2005 and 11% in 2006, indicated that they found the postings interfered with their use of the course site. Some students suggested in comments that the postings needed to be changed more frequently or removed after a few days without change. This reinforces the importance of keeping library blog content fresh.

The vast majority of students noticed the library postings, but did they respond to them? Traffic at the actual library blog was consistently light. The postings were viewed an average of four times per day during the semester. Among the students, for both 2005 and 2006, 50% reported reading at least one blog post at least once during the semester. Of that number, 15% in 2005 and 20% in 2006 reported attending a library event or taking some other action as a result of reading a blog post in their courseware. That may seem rather inconsequential, but because these students learned about a library program they would likely otherwise miss, it is actually substantial in terms of reaching members of our community. If the blog was used in 100 courses rather than 20, the figure of 15% begins to have a greater impact on stimulating the use of the library's services and resources and participation at our events.

Despite the moderate success of the integration of the library blog into courseware at my institution, considering that 75% in 2005 and 84% in 2006 indicated they thought the library should continue to push the postings to their courseware sites, there is reason for cautious optimism about library blogs. When asked how they prefer to receive news and information about the library, students still prefer e-mail by a wide margin. It may be premature to assume our users prefer blogs over traditional methods. "Send feeds to courseware" was second only to e-mail and was preferred over other communication options such as library newsletter and paper announcements, which may be a potential cause for optimism.

Perhaps the most significant finding is that of all respondents, a mere 5% in 2005 and 12% in 2006 indicated they would voluntarily subscribe to the library blog. This suggests that it is unrealistic for libraries of any type to expect that large numbers of their user community would voluntarily subscribe to a library blog. It further suggests that it seems inefficient and questionable for the library administration to allocate resources for a library blog in order to reach such a small portion of the user community. Clearly, making use of the available technology to push the blog content out to the user community is a better way to get them reading the library blog.

Tips for Successful Library Blogging

It is easy to discount the findings of my experiment as inconsequential. So what if the library blog is not the product of thoughtful assessment about whether it makes sense for the user community? And so what if those users may know little about blogs or the technology required to best use them? Why bother with such concerns, especially when experts are touting the value of library blogs? As far as experimentation with new technology and services go, library blogs are fairly risk-free. Other than time, there is little cost. Who cares if hardly anyone reads it or has an aggregator they can use to subscribe to the library blog? A library blog causes no harm, and it really is fun to create and produce.

However, a poorly conceived and executed library blog can do more harm than good, and library blogging will grow into a burdensome chore if it becomes apparent that few users are paying attention. Library blogs that are heavily promoted and then deliver bland content, or that are rarely updated, do reflect badly upon the library, not unlike a dismal library Web site. But with some thoughtful planning for pushing blog content to users, a library blog can be a positive, rewarding experience for all parties. There are a number of ways in which to accomplish that goal.

Update Regularly

Think about a well-respected blog. Chances are it is one easily depended upon on for daily or near-daily updated content. Whether we read them for news or commentary, blogs become part of our daily routine of reading when we anticipate the delivery of new ideas and information. A library blog should be no different. Keeping it fresh is critical for its success. Unless there is a commitment to update the blog every day or so, reconsider the idea of creating one.

Quality Content

By its very nature, the content of a library blog will rarely rise to the levels of the most controversial, entertaining, or snappily-written blogs. While library blogs may be content-challenged, there is no reason they cannot rise above a repetitive blur of mundane announcements and news items that are of little interest to anyone outside the library. A natural advantage in the library's favor is knowledge of who the users are and what they need to achieve success. Strong familiarity with a particular assignment or community event of importance is a good example. If librarians can provide news, information, and ideas that focus on what is important to users rather than the library's interests, then there is an opportunity to grab the users' interest and keep them looking for more of the same.

Quick Completion

Design and execute the library blog with the intent of completing it in approximately 15 minutes per day. Most librarians lack the luxury of time for blog updates and maintenance. If library blogging becomes a daily search for something to say, the process can take far more time than expected. A library blog is not a personal blog. Avoid commentary and long explanations. Users will be drawn to brief, pithy postings. If more content is needed, put it elsewhere, perhaps on an explanatory Web page. Involving multiple staff can help, but having them feed blog items to a single poster will give the content a more consistent writing style.

Content Policies

Consistency can be especially important for team blogs where several library staff members contribute to the blog. In these situations, the blog contributors, with oversight from the library administration, should determine in advance what is considered acceptable content. It could be limited to strictly library-related news and information. It could be broader, perhaps including information about community events. It could be broader yet, perhaps including news stories about libraries other than one's own. The primary issue to avoid is having any individual blogger take a drastically different approach to content. It may be that personal information will be off limits. Content objectives should be determined in advance. To allow for flexibility, a system should be devised for reviewing questionable content.

Review Library Blogs

Before beginning a library blog, it is advisable to review a variety of other library blogs. Examine them for style and content decisions.

73

This can help the library staff determine what approach to blogging will work best for them and their community. It can also help in setting content policies.

Unforeseen Benefits

Following the tips listed above may help produce better blog content while keeping it manageable for staff, but blogging to courseware requires the added element of sensitivity. At all times remember that the library is but a guest within the course site. Students are there for course-related information, not to learn about the library. The blog postings need to be short, informative, and eye-catching without overwhelming the main course page. This requires a combination of good headlines, concentrated information in the least number of words, and regularly updated postings. It is also important to provide a content mix that appeals to a diverse user community. Drawing too heavily, for example, on news of interest to students in one discipline is sure to alienate other segments of the community.

It is all harder than it sounds, but it can be worth the effort. In my academic community, blogging to courseware has produced the added benefit of sparking faculty interest in RSS technology. Several faculty members expressed interest in wanting to understand how blogs, RSS, and news aggregators can help students learn about their disciplines. For example, a science professor wanted to feed postings from a blog about the everyday, practical applications of scientific principles into his chemistry course. A global perspectives course instructor wanted the students to see new feeds from the *Financial Times of London*. These faculty members thought RSS feeds could be a good way to help students make connections between the course content and the world beyond the classroom. With so many mainstream media publications providing RSS feeds, it is now easier than ever to discover feeds appropriate for a specific course. This growing interest in RSS technologies prompted the Gutman Library to offer workshops on these topics. The unexpected benefit of blogging to courseware was an emerging role for the library as the campus leader in creating awareness about and education in the rapidly evolving technologies of blogging, news aggregation, social networking, and personalization of search.

Conclusion

While this chapter might seem somewhat biased against new technologies and progressive experimentation with them, be assured that I understand the importance of exploring new technologies to discover practical applications that benefit library users. I also respect colleagues who experiment with blogs and other new technologies, but it is still reasonable to question whether they are doing enough to research the concrete benefits of applying them to library environments. Librarians should apply a test before they adopt and apply any new technology to service delivery or marketing. Does it enable us to achieve our service outcomes for constituents, and are we able to measure our degree of success? As it applies to library blogs, if there is no demonstrable advantage as measured by its ability to achieve service outcomes, then library administrators should question if staff time and resources allocated to this activity are helping to achieve stated outcomes or are wasting time that could be better spent on other endeavors. It is critical to question how and why blogging technology is an appropriate application for your library in terms of benefits for users, just as any educator should question how the integration of a new technology is going to benefit learners.

So consider the options. You can create a library blog, make it publicly accessible, and hope someone will bother to read it. Or, by pushing your blog content to your users, you can take steps to ensure that the time and effort put into each posting results in connecting with someone in your user community. The latter option seems far more sensible. What makes it even more so, as this chapter has detailed, is that using RSS-to-Javascript converters makes this easy to do at no cost to the library. When you think about it, this is one decision that is really easy to make.

2006 Survey Questions and Response Data

01. I have noticed the headlines (we refer to them here as "postings") about Gutman Library appearing on the announcements page of my Blackboard Course Site (at least one if you have several this semester).

Answer	Count	Percent
No	26	36.11%
Yes	46	63.89%

02. During the spring 2006 semester, I clicked on these postings to read them:

Answer	Count
1–5 times this semester	19
6–10 times this semester	3
Never clicked on any this semester	50

03. How helpful or useful have you found these postings this semester?

Answer	Count	Percent
2	20	28.57%
3	19	27.14%
4	31	44.29%

04. Did the addition of library news postings to your course announcement page interfere with access to your instructor's announcements or in any other way interfere with your use of the course site?

Answer	Count	Percent
1	2	2.86%
2	5	7.14%
3	13	18.57%
4	50	71.43%

(cont'd.)

2006 Survey Questions and Response Data *(Continued)*

05. I would like Gutman Library to continue to add the postings from their Library WebLog, "Get It At Gutman," to my Blackboard Course Sites.

Answer	Count	Percent
Maybe	48	67.61%
No	12	16.90%
Yes	11	15.49%

06. Indicate how you prefer to receive news and information from Gutman Library (choose more than one if it applies).

Answer	Count
Add posts to Blackboard Announcement Page	20
Have faculty member tell me about library events	13
Monthly Newsletter from Library	18
Other, Please Specify:	6
Receive paper announcements	4

06. Other.

Answer	Count	Percent
add an announcement section on the gutman Web site	1	16.67%
add to homepage	1	16.67%
bullet point on the Web site	1	16.67%
e-mail to let us know they are in blackboard	1	16.67%
I for one never read the gutman newsletters	1	16.67%
on the Web site	1	16.67%

(cont'd.)

77

2006 Survey Questions and Response Data *(Continued)*

07. Did you attend any library programs or events or take other action (e.g., going to the library Web site; using the library when you might not have in the past) as a result of reading a posting?

Answer	Count	Percent
No	57	79.17%
Yes	15	20.83%

08. I currently read Weblogs (blogs). Please select the most appropriate response from the dropbox.

Answer	Count	Percent
I don't know what blogs are	13	19.12%
I know what blogs are but I don't follow any of them	47	69.12%
Yes, I currently follow 1–10 blogs	8	11.76%

09. Do you currently use a news aggregator (e.g., Bloglines) to capture feeds from blogs. Please select the most appropriate response from the dropbox.

Answer	Count	Percent
I do not know what a news aggregator is	48	70.59%
I know what a news aggregator is, but do not use one	18	26.47%
Yes, I currently use a news aggregator to subscribe to blogs	2	2.94%

(cont'd.)

78

2006 Survey Questions and Response Data *(Continued)*

10. You saw the type of information Gutman Library communicates with its Weblog "Get It At Gutman." Would you voluntarily subscribe to the library Weblog, or bookmark it? In other words, would you use the library's Weblog for information about the library (if you weren't getting the postings in your Blackboard Course Site)?

Answer	Count	Percent
I would prefer to see the postings in my course site rather than subscribe to the actual library Weblog	28	39.44%
No, I would not subscribe to or otherwise follow the library's Weblog.	34	47.89%
Yes, I would subscribe to or otherwise follow the library's Weblog	9	12.68%

11. Please choose the frequency that best indicates how often you visited or used the Blackboard Course Site that contained the library Weblog postings.

Answer	Count	Percent
1–5 time per week (moderate usage)	17	23.61%
5–10 times per month (low usage)	4	5.56%
6–10 times per week (high usage)	9	12.50%
Less than 5 times per month (rare usage)	36	50.00%
Other	6	8.33%

Editor's Note: Parts of this chapter were previously published in "Where The Readers Are: Blogging To Courseware." *NetConnect* (*Supplement to Library Journal* 130(17): 8–13, October 15, 2005. The author appreciates the permission received from *Library Journal* to reprint this content here.

References

Best, Jo. 2005. "RSS: 98% of Surfers Shun It." *WebWatch*. http://networks.silicon.com/Webwatch/0,39024667,39150835,00.htm (accessed 12 March 2005).

Bausch, Suzy, and Tracy Yen. 2005. "One in 10 Weblog Readers Personalizes Content with RSS Feeds." *Nielsen NetRatings*. http://www.nielsen-netratings.com/pr/pr_050815 (accessed 12 March 2005).

Coffman, Steve and Linda Arret. To Chat Or Not to Chat—Taking Another Look at Virtual Reference: Part I. *Searcher* (1 Jul 2004):38–46.

Coffman, Steve and Linda Arret. To Chat Or Not to Chat—Taking Another Look at Virtual Reference: Part II. *Searcher* (1 Sep 2004):49–56.

de Rosa, Cathy et. al. 2006. *College Students' Perceptions of Libraries and Information Resources*. Dublin, OH: OCLC Online Computer Library Center. http://www.oclc.org/reports/perceptionscollege.htm (accessed 30 March 2006).

Wiemer, Kris. 2005. "Integrating RSS Feeds into Your Course Management System." *Low-Threshold Application Site*. 2 February 2005. http://zircon.mcli.dist.maricopa.edu/lta/archives/lta44.php (accessed 18 March 2005)

Notes

Notes

82

Chapter 5

An Introduction to Podcasting for Librarians

John Iliff and Tyler Rousseau

Abstract
Podcasting has much to offer libraries. This chapter explores the possibilities of podcasting by examining the current state of the technology, identifying the creators and viewers of podcasts, and teaching the reader how to create his or her own podcast. The authors discuss the technical aspects of creating the audio files and RSS feed. Finally, several exemplary library podcasts are described and evaluated.

83

About the Authors
John Iliff (1953–2006) Until his death in May 2006, John Iliff was Library Technology Development Consultant for PALINET in Philadelphia, PA, and was well known for his many presentations on various areas of technology, most recently podcasting and RSS. He wrote many articles on technology as well as a foreword to Elizabeth Thomsen's *Reference and Collection Development on the Internet: A How-To-Do-It Manual for Librarians.* John was a contributing author and technical reviewer to the book *The Internet Unleashed.* In 1992, along with Jean Armour Polly, he co-founded and co-moderated PUBLIB, the first worldwide electronic discussion list for public librarians. Previously, John had worked as a reference librarian at Pinellas Park Public Library in Florida; as librarian and assistant professor for the Consortium Library at the

University of Alaska Anchorage; and as reference librarian and associate professor at College of Staten Island, New York (CUNY).

Tyler Rousseau is a young-adult (YA) librarian with the Ocean County Library System. He serves as a member-at-large on the New Jersey Library Association's Information Technology section. Staying true to his passion of working with teens, much of Tyler's research revolves around gaming, social networks, research methods, and teens' general interest in technology. Tyler is also an author of his own blog and has posted several articles on podcasting and technological trends in libraries.

Introduction

As we saw in Chapters 1 and 2, RSS feeds can give library patrons easy, flexible access to frequently updated collections of information. We once may have printed a list of index subscriptions or placed lists of databases on our Web site, but now we can provide patrons that same information—and more—in a far more supple, user-centered way.

Podcasting extends RSS to include sound files as well as text, allowing libraries to provide that same flexible access to collections of audio recordings. The basic approach is the same: like RSS feeds that link to external files, podcasts describe individual audio files and arrange them into a channel to which users can subscribe. When new content is added to the podcast, users can automatically download it and listen to it on their personal computers or digital audio players.

From the user's perspective, then, podcasts resemble very deliberately programmed radio stations. From the provider's perspective, podcasts are refreshingly simple to create and maintain. Libraries are increasingly using podcasts to provide wider access to lectures and storytime sessions, library orientation materials, and bibliographic instruction. This chapter describes the technology behind podcasting, provides a detailed tutorial on how to create your own podcast, and concludes with a quick look at some well established library podcasts.

Understanding Podcasts

Behind each podcast is a collection of audio recordings. In most cases, these recordings are stored in a compressed file format, which allows large audio files to be greatly reduced in size while retaining reasonable fidelity. This is an especially pressing concern for users of portable digital audio players, which necessarily provide less storage capacity than standard personal computers. The MP3 (short for Moving Pictures Experts Group-Layer 3) format file compression is the most popular of these formats, though others—such as OGG Vorbis—have increasingly devoted followings.

These collections of audio recordings are organized into RSS feeds using markup similar to that discussed in chapters 1 and 2. Users access podcasts via programs called podcatchers. Many podcatchers are available. Some, like iTunes' podcatching service, are built into other applications, while others are dedicated, stand-alone products. Among the most popular standalone podcatchers is the open-source, cross-platform Juice (http://juicereceiver. sourceforge.net/). In the Figure 5.1, we see several podcasts in Juice's upper window, with the files associated with one of those podcasts in the lower window.

85

The term "podcasting" is a synecdoche. Users need not own an iPod to listen to podcasts. Podcasts themselves can be accessed from any computer connected to the Internet, and MP3 files can be played on any suitable digital audio player. These include iPods and other portable audio players as well as personal computers.

Podcasting Today

Finding Podcasts

Because RSS files are plain text and accessed via Web servers, most are indexed by major search engines. Keyword searches via a search engine such as Google will return links to podcasts via RSS xml files (in the case of Google, more accurate returns will result when searches are limited to the xml format).

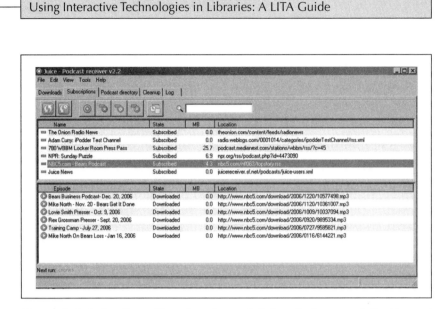

Figure 5.1: Juice Page Showing Several Subscriptions and the Recent Contents of One Podcast

Another technique for locating podcasts is via topically arranged hierarchical podcast indexes. Topical categories tend to start as broad subject areas such as business, education, or media. Each topic is subdivided into more precise subtopics, and most hierarchies are apt to be no more than three or four subtopics deep. Podcast directories include www.PodcastAlley.com, www.Podcast.net,www.podcastingnews.com, and www.indiepodder.org. Many podcatchers provide built-in access to podcast directories.

Keyword searching of podcasts is available on Web-based services via letter-by-letter access to the transcribed textual content of podcasts. Two noteworthy services that provide this type of retrieval are Podzinger and Podscope. Each has limitations in terms of searching sophistication as well as accuracy in transcribing.

Who Is Listening?

In June 2005, according to a survey by the Pew Internet and American Life Project, more than six million adults in the United States had downloaded and listened to podcasts on portable digital devices. This may seem like a large number of listeners, but the percentage of adults in the United States listening to podcasts as reported by the Pew Project is less than 2%. By April 2006, a study by Forrester Research found that 3% of U.S. consumers had listened to podcasts, but that only 700,000 were regular listeners. The Forrester study predicted that regular listeners of podcasts would increase to 12 million by 2010 (or about 6% of the population) (Fildes, 2005). Those who listen to podcasts, according to the Pew study, tend to be wealthier, better educated, and younger (Raine and Madden, 2005).

Who Is Podcasting?

Many podcasts are private efforts undertaken by individuals or small groups. Increasingly, though, many commercial entities are embracing podcasts. One of the first major corporations to develop podcasts was General Motors, which uses the audio files to highlight its product line. IBM recently introduced podcasts for internal communications to save on conference calls. The Disney Corporation uses podcasts to promote its theme parks and other services. A Disneyland Anniversary program in August 2005 had over 75,000 downloads (Hopkins, 2005).

87

Media outlets have aggressively developed podcasts in recent years. National Public Radio has an extensive directory of podcasts reproduced from broadcasts, as well as programs created exclusively in the podcast format. Major news channels such as ABC, CNN, NBC, FOX, and the BBC feature ever-increasing numbers of podcasts derived from television, print, and radio sources. Increasing numbers of local media outlets also produce podcasts on a range of topics. Journal publishers are following suit: Nature Publishing Group, for example, offers a weekly program with expanded information based on articles from its flagship journal *Nature* (nature.com/nature/podcast/index.html).

In the public sector, many government entities have embraced podcasting. These include elected officials, increasing numbers of whom are using podcasts as a new avenue for communicating with their constituents. President Bush's weekly radio addresses are now syndicated as podcasts, and federal agencies have begun to make use of the technology. The Free Government Information (FGI) Website includes an excellent directory of government podcasts at http://freegovinfo.info/node/174.

This surge in popularity is due largely to the ease with which new podcasts can be created. Recording audio onto a computer is a simple and inexpensive process, and creating the RSS code requires no advanced programming skills. Podcast-hosting sites such as podomatic.com will even generate the code for you.

Creating a Podcast

Podcasts are composed of two elements: the audio files and the markup describing them. This section describes the creation of those components and the assembly of a podcast. Even if your library chooses to use a service like podomatic, it is helpful to know exactly what goes into each podcast's production.

Recording the Audio File: Computer and Microphone

In recent years, personal computers have become popular tools for recording audio of all kinds. Music for many films and television shows, for instance, is written and recorded on elaborately outfitted, astonishingly expensive computers. Luckily, podcasts require nothing more than a computer, a microphone, and freely available software.

A standard desktop microphone, available for $10–$15 at most consumer electronics stores, is sufficient for podcasting. Use of a standard analog desktop microphone requires a special jack on your computer designed to accept a microphone's signal and amplify it appropriately; this jack is standard on many personal computers and is usually clearly marked. Microphones send a very low-level signal that must be boosted to line level before it is recorded. Plugging an analog microphone into a line in jack will result in a faint, distorted signal. Desktop microphones with USB connectors also are available.

Improving Audio Quality

Higher audio quality can be achieved with a better microphone and/or a better audio interface for your computer.

Basic dynamic microphones, which create their own electrical current, can be bought for $70 or less. Condenser microphones, which generally provide greater fidelity than dynamics while exhibiting much greater sensitivity to ambient noise, are often a bit more expensive. Condensers also require a constant supply of electrical current, known as "phantom power."

USB- and Firewire-based audio interfaces provide much better pre-amplification for microphone- and instrument-level sources, and much better analog-digital converters than most standard computer hardware. Many also provide power to condenser microphones. Their prices generally start at $250 or $300.

Once you have chosen a computer and microphone, you will need a program with which to record your audio signal. Audacity (audacity.sourceforge.net) is one mature, highly regarded open-source audio recording/editing application (Figure 5.2). It comes with thorough documentation, which will help you to begin recording in minutes.

Recording the Audio File: Public Address System
If you wish to record a presentation delivered over a PA system, two basic approaches are available to you. The first is to use the approach described above by placing a second microphone near the speaker and routing it to a computer. In this case, it may be wise to buy an inexpensive extension cord for your microphone, so the recording may be overseen by someone seated away from the speaker. The signal may weaken a bit if forced to travel a longer distance, so be sure to test this setup before recording a live event.

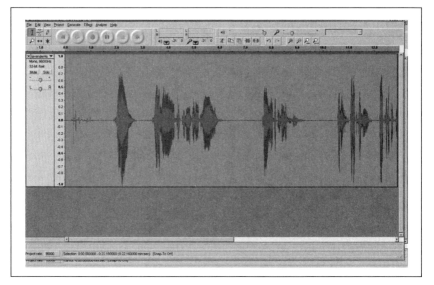

Figure 5.2: A Single Vocal Track on Audacity

If such an approach is not feasible, you may want to investigate the possibility of recording directly from your PA system. In this scenario, the computer would receive its audio signal not from a microphone, but from the PA system's Line Out. This may require an inexpensive adapter: nearly all computers use 1/8" TRS (Tip-Ring-Sleeve) jacks, while the PA system's line out jack is likely to be an RCA (common on home stereo equipment) or XLR (circular with three pins, used on studio microphones and related equipment and to carry balanced signals over long distances). Regardless of the connections used, the signal's level will remain the same: you may safely connect an XLR line out to a TRS line in.

Remember that the PA system's Line Out is providing a much stronger signal than a microphone. If you send a line-level signal to a microphone input, your computer will still try to boost the signal, leading at best to a harshly distorted signal. When testing a new connection, it is always a good idea to turn all volume settings to 0, and to gradually raise the signal until it reaches its desired level.

Editing the Audio File

If you make a few minor mistakes while recording, do not worry. Audacity will display your audio's waveform, and you will be able to edit it freely. You can cut out too-long silences or extra syllables, raise or lower the overall volume, and move entire passages from one point to another. You can even copy audio from one Audacity project to another—this makes it easy to reuse common introductions and closings for your podcast episodes.

Along with its built-in editing functions, Audacity includes a number of plug-in effects and the ability to add as many more as you choose. An effect can be ornamental—reverb and chorus effects add distinctly identifiable qualities to the original signal—but it can also be more subtly corrective. Two popular corrective effects are equalization and compression.

Equalization is familiar to anyone who has adjusted the treble and bass knobs on a stereo: it simply raises or lowers certain frequencies. The equalization (EQ) plug-ins in Audacity provide a greater degree of control than the standard treble/bass approach. They can significantly improve a recording's clarity and character.

Compression attenuates the loudest parts of a signal by a specified ratio, often accompanied by a subsequent boost of the signal's overall volume. It makes the loudest parts softer and, if needed, makes the softest parts louder. As such, it can be an invaluable tool for improving vocal recordings, which often suffer from inconsistent volume levels.

Along with its native plug-ins, Audacity can host VST (Virtual Studio Technology) effects. VST is a wildly popular standard for creating virtual effects and instruments, and many impressive VSTs are available for free. KVR Audio (www.kvraudio.com) provides an excellent VST clearinghouse.

Incorporating Multiple Audio Files

Audacity also provides for multitrack recording. This allows several individual tracks to be mixed together in one file; background music, for instance, is added by multitracking. In the example

91

below, our spoken-word track is backed by a simple rhythmic accompaniment. Each track can be manipulated independently in Audacity. In Figure 5.3, we have highlighted a portion of our background track and applied a fade-out effect. When all your tracks have been added and adjusted to your liking, Audacity will export the result as a single file, mixing all tracks together.

Saving the Audio File

After you have edited your file to your satisfaction, you will need to export it in your chosen format. Due to its popularity and near-universality as of this writing, MP3 is the wisest choice for podcasts. The MP3 encoding/decoding standard is licensed by Fraunhofer IIS, and while its use by libraries creating podcasts is generally accepted as legal, MP3 encoding cannot be included in a freely distributed application like Audacity. The Help files included in Audacity describe the steps needed to create an MP3 file from your recording. Once you have created the MP3 file, move it to the server on which it will be tested or deployed.

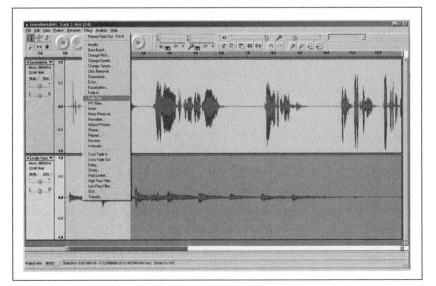

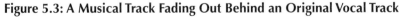

Figure 5.3: A Musical Track Fading Out Behind an Original Vocal Track

Creating the RSS Feed

Now that you have created an audio file, the only step left is to describe that file in an RSS feed. This step need not be done entirely by hand. Several excellent RSS generators are available via the Web.

Here is what will appear in a basic podcast RSS feed:

<?xml version="1.0"?>: **Identifies the feed as an XML document.**
<rss version="2.0">: **Identifies the feed as an RSS document.**

<channel>: **All descriptive information is enclosed in the <channel> tag. The next five tags describe your channel.**
<title>Your First Podcast</title>
<link>http://www.yourlibrary.org/podcasts/</link>
<description>The first podcast produced by your library</description>
<language>en-us</language>
<copyright>Copyright 2006 Your Library</copyright>

<item>: **Each mp3 file is described as an item.**

These four tags describe a single file:
<title>How We Wrote Our Podcast Feed</title> -
<link>http://www.yourlibrary.org/podcasts/first/</link>
<description>The fascinating story of how we created the document behind this podcast</description>
<enclosure url="http://www.yourlibrary.org/podcasts/first/001.mp3" length="872470" type="audio/mpeg"/>: **Identifies the location, size, and type of the first item's file.**
</item>

<item>
[title, link, description and enclosure tags for the next item go here]
</item>

</channel>
</rss>

iTunes adds several custom tags, which are necessary if you wish iTunes to carry your podcast in its online inventory, but

93

which are not required for simple playback within iTunes. Many RSS generators add these fields. If you wish to write your RSS feed by hand, consult www.apple.com/itunes/store/podcaststech-specs.html for more information.

Validating the RSS Feed

After saving the RSS feed to your server, you should check it for proper form and syntax. This process, known as validation, is optional, but it is a simple and cost-free way of tracking down any errors that might have crept into your RSS file. Simply go feedvalidator.org and enter the location of your feed. If your feed needs work, you will be given instructions on how to proceed. If it is valid, you will be greeted with the notice in Figure 5.4.

As you create more audio files for your podcast, simply upload them to your server and add to your RSS feed as necessary.

We now know what podcasts are, how they are used, and how they are created. But what is their role in the library world? We conclude this chapter with a look at how librarians are using podcasts.

Library Podcasts

In early 2005, librarian podcast pioneer Greg Schwartz created one of the first librarian-oriented podcasts. Schwartz is Circulation

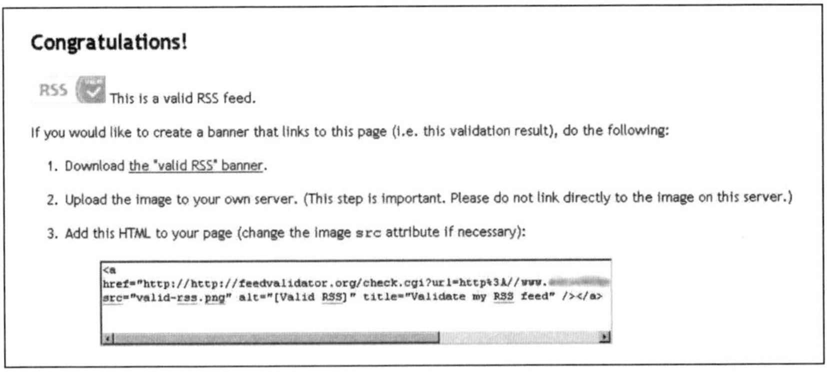

Congratulations!

RSS ☑ This is a valid RSS feed.

If you would like to create a banner that links to this page (i.e. this validation result), do the following:

1. Download the "valid RSS" banner.

2. Upload the image to your own server. (This step is important. Please do not link directly to the image on this server.)

3. Add this HTML to your page (change the image src attribute if necessary):

```
<a
href="http://http://feedvalidator.org/check.cgi?url=http%3A//www.
src="valid-rss.png" alt="[Valid RSS]" title="Validate my RSS feed" /></a>
```

Figure 5.4: Feed Validation

Support Supervisor for the Louisville Free Public Library in Kentucky. His podcasts, many of which are geared toward introducing new technologies to fellow librarians, are regularly featured in his personal Open Stacks blog at http://openstacks.net/os/.

Another pioneering effort has been led by Chris Kretz, Instructor/Reference Librarian at the Dowling College Library in New York. His series of podcasts, titled Omnibus, are artfully produced programs that incorporate music, poetry readings, interviews, and even audio documentaries (www.dowling.edu/library/ newsblog/podcasts.asp?id=14). The music is derived from the Podshow Podsafe Music Network, which contains music files copyrighted under provisions of Creative Commons (Figure 5.5). Many of the podcast interviewees are faculty from the Dowling campus.

Just as well executed, but with a more traditional focus on library services, is the Arizona State University Libraries podcast series at www.asu.edu/ lib/podcasts/. Titled the Library Channel, these polished programs include components of library instruction,

95

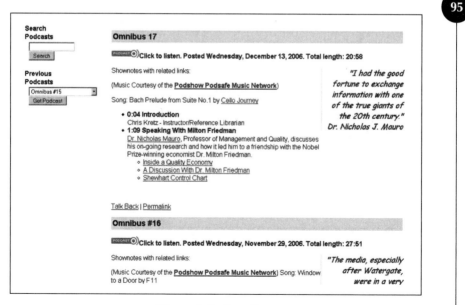

Figure 5.5: Omnibus

lectures by staff and guests, and also include both audio and video files. Other noteworthy university library podcasts include those at Curtin University in Australia, which features a tour of the library (http://library.curtin.edu.au/podcast/); Western Kentucky University, which has an extensive series of lectures on a variety of topics (http://www.wku.edu/Library/podcast/index.html); and the Johns Hopkins University Sheridan Libraries, which present pithy podcasts for library orientation and instruction (www.library.jhu. edu/podcasts/index.html).

Several public libraries also are creating podcasts, frequently with young adults and children as the target audience. In some instances, young adults are creating the podcasts. Topics tend to range from book talks, to book reviews, to storytelling. Public libraries making creative use of podcasts include the Lansing Public Library in Michigan (http://www.lansing.lib.il.us/podcast.htm), the Orange County Library System in Florida (www.ocls.info/ Programs/podcastAndRSS.asp?bhcp=1), the Kankakee, IL Public Library (www.kankakee. lib.il.us/podtext.htm), and the Thomas Ford Memorial Library in Western Springs, IL, whose *Click-A-Story* program (Figure 5.6) features material written by young authors (http://www.fordlibrary.org/clickastory/).

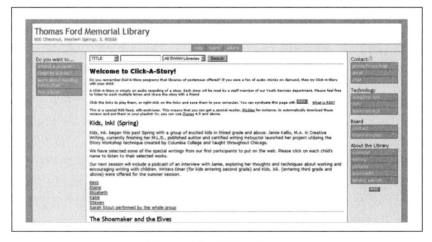

Figure 5.6: Click-A-Story

Conclusion

As of this writing (spring 2006), a search on Google of the xml file type and the word podcast reaped over 900,000 returns. As digital media become more popular and more portable, libraries have a golden opportunity to fulfill their traditional missions via new technologies.

References and Further Reading

Fildes, Jonathan. 2006. "Podcast Numbers Cut Through Hype." *BBC News*, April 10. http://news.bbc.co.uk/2/hi/technology/4885010.stm.

Hopkins, Jamie S. Corporations Go Off a-Podcasting. *Baltimore Sun* (11 Dec 2005): sec. C. Kreider Eash, Esther. Podcasting 101 for K–12 Librarians. *Computers in Libraries* (April 2006):16–20.

Raine, Lee, and Mary Madden. 2005. *Memo: Podcasting*. Pew Internet and American Life Project.

Rojas, Peter. "iTunes 4.9 Adding Support for Podcasts." *Engadget* (23 May 2005). www.engadget.com/2005/05/23/itunes-4-9-adding-support-for-podcasts/.

Notes

Index

A

aggregators, RSS
  examples of, 19
  RSS Creator and, 8–9
  user self-aggregation, 28–29
alerting service
  See RSS Creator
American Libraries, 61
applications, library, 17
applications, RSS, 20–22
Arizona State University Libraries
  podcast series, 95–96
Arret, Linda, 60, 61
Audacity
  editing audio file in, 91
  multitracking, 91–92
  recording audio file in, 89
  saving audio file in, 92
  track on, 90
audience, 86–87
audio file
  editing, 91
  multitracking, 91–92
  for podcast, 84, 85
  recording, 88–91
  RSS feed, creation of, 93–94
audio quality, 89
authentication, database, 32

B

Bausch, Suzy, 63
Bell, Steven J., x, 59–79
Best, Jo, 63
Biz Wiki
  challenges of, 52–54

Biz Wiki *(cont'd.)*
  content, adding/editing, 49–52
  content of, 45–47
  organization/search features, 47–49
  setting up, 43–45
  usage of, 52
Blackboard, 32
Blackboard Instructional Designers
  discussion list, 65
Blended Librarian's Online Learning
  Community, 60
blogs, 31
  See also library blogs
Boeninger, Chad F., x, 39–54
Bush, George W., 87–88

C

California State University San Marcos,
  5, 9
Cervone, H. Frank, xi
chat, 60–61
Christensen, Heather, 29
Cites & Insights (Crawford), 61
Coffman, Steve, 60, 61
*College Students' Perceptions of Library
  and Information Resources* study
  (Online Computer Library Center),
  63
compression, 91
computer, 85, 88–90
condenser microphone, 89
Connotea, 33
content
  of Biz Wiki, 45–47
  of library blog, 72–73, 74

content *(cont'd.)*
 new, staying current with, 18
 new, user notification of, 2–3
 sharing via RSS, 12
 Wiki, 44–45, 49–52
converter, RSS-to-Javascript, 64–68, 75
corporations, podcasting and, 87
courseware
 blogging to, benefits of, 74–75
 blogging to, experiment/reactions to,
  69–71
 RSS-to-Javascript Converter for
  blog, 64–68
Cox, John, 2
Crawford, Walt, 61
cross-reference, 48–49
Curtin University, Australia, 96

D
database providers, 3–4
databases, online research, 18
databases, subscription
 platform, 22–25
 RSS applications, 20–22
 RSS feed/Web page integration, 25–26
 RSS for, 19–20, 35
 user authentication, 32
Disney Corporation, 87
"Do you believe in Web 2.0?" (EPS
 Focus Report), 33
Dowling College Library, 95
Drexel University College of
 Information Science and
 Technology, 59
Drumm, Michelle, 34

E
editing, audio file, 91
effects, podcast, 91
Einstein, Albert, 19
e-mail, 2–3
EPS Focus Report, 33
EPS Insights, 28–29
equalization, 91

Ex Libris, 5, 12
export, of podcast audio file, 92

F
faculty
 library blog and, 69–70, 74
 RSS and, 12
 Wiki and, 53–54
Feed2JS converter, 25–26, 65–68
Fildes, Jonathan, 87
filtering, user, 28, 35
find
 See search
Forrester Research, 63, 87
Free Government Information (FGI)
 Website, 88

G
General Motors, 87
Get It At Gutman (Gutman Library
 Weblog), 64–71, 74–75
Google, 28, 40
government sector, podcasting by, 87–88

H
Hanson, Kathlene, xi
Hanson, Terry, 2
high school students, 28
Hopkins, Jamie S., 87
Horne, Angelina K., 2
hosting services, Wiki, 44
HTML page, 64–68
hype cycle, ix

I
IBM, 87
Iliff, John, x–xi, 83–97
"Information Industry User Habits"
 (Outsell), 26–27
instructional content, of Wiki, 46–47
*Integrating Information Resources:
 Principles, Technologies, and
 Approaches* (Christensen and
 Tenant), 29

"Integrating RSS Feeds into Your Course management System" (Wiemer), 66
Internet
    search vs. "subscribe and filter", 28
    Web-based subject guides, 39–41
Internet Protocol (IP) address, 32
iPod, 85
ISSN queries, 7
iTunes, 85, 93–94
Ive, Jonathan, 19

J
jack, 88
Javascript, RSS-to-Javascript Converter, 64–68
Johns Hopkins University Sheridan Libraries, 96
journal feeds, 2–4
journals
    indexing, RSS Creator and, 11
    RSS Creator and, 5–7
    RSS feeds and, 2
Juice, 85, 86

K
Kankakee, IL Public Library, 96
The Kept-Up Academic Librarian blog (Steven J. Bell), 60, 62
key word search, 86
Kretz, Chris, 95
Kristensen, Terry L., 2

L
Lansing Public Library, 96
Law, John, x, 17–35
learning management systems, 25, 31–32
library
    application of RSS feeds, 17, 30–32
    new technology and, 60–62, 75
    podcasts of, 94–96
    RSS adoption by, ix–x

library blogs
    benefits of, 74–75
    conclusion about, 75
    in courseware sites, 64
    in courseware sites, reactions to, 70–71
    new technology, use of, 59
    promises/pitfalls of, 61–62
    RSS to Javascript Converters, 64–68
    student experiment, 69–70
    survey questions/response data, 76–79
    tips for, 71–74
    user community and, 62–64
    virtual reference movement and, 60–61
Library Channel (Arizona State University Libraries podcast), 95–96
library instruction sessions, 40
library mission, 26–27
library podcasts, 94–96
library services, 29–32
Library Voice blog (Chad Boeninger), 39
line out, 90
links, 48–49
listeners, podcast, 86–87
Louisville Free Public Library, 95
Lucene, 5–6

M
Madden, Mary, 87
MARCit service, 5, 12
Maricopa Community College, 25
media outlets, 87
MediaWiki, 44–45, 52
MetaLib, 7
microphone, 88–90
MP3 (Moving Pictures Experts Group-Layer 3) format, 85, 92
multitracking, 91–92

N
National Public Radio, 87
Nature Publishing Group, 33, 87
New American Oxford Dictionary, ix

New Jersey Library Association's
Information Technology section, 84
news aggregators, 63–64
Nielsen Associates, 63

O

Ocean County Library System, 84
Ohio University Alden Library, 39
Ohio University Libraries, 41–54
Omnibus podcasts (Chris Kretz), 95
Online Computer Library Center, 63
Open Stacks blog (Greg Schwartz), 95
Orange County Library System, Florida,
96
organization, of Wiki, 47–49
Outsell, 26–27, 35

P

PA (public address) system, 89–90
PALINET, 83
PALINET Technology Conversations
Podcast Series, xi
pathfinders
See research guide
Paul J. Gutman Library at Philadelphia
University
blog of, 64–71
blogging to courseware, benefits of,
74–75
Steven J. Bell of, 59–60
survey questions/response data,
63–64, 76–79
pbWiki hosting service, 44
Pew Internet and American Life Project,
86–87
plug-ins, Audacity, 91
podcast, creation of, 88–94
audio quality, 89
editing audio file, 91
multitracking, 91–92
recording audio file, 88–90
RSS feed, creation of, 93–94
RSS feed, validation of, 94
saving audio file, 92

podcast directories, 86
podcasting
author information, 83–84
creating podcast, 88–94
description of, 84–85
finding podcasts, 85–86
library podcasts, examples of, 94–96
listeners, 86–87
popularity of, 97
who is using, 87–88
podcatchers, 85
Podscope, 86
Podshow Podsafe Music Network, 95
Podzinger, 86
Polly, Jean Armour, 83
predefined feeds, 21
ProQuest
PhD dissertation collection, 20
RSS and, 34
RSS feeds aggregation with, 19
ProQuest Information and Learning,
17–18
proxy servers, 33
PUBLIB, 83
public address (PA) system, 89–90
publication feed, 21
publishers, RSS feeds and, 3–4

R

Raine, Lee, 87
Really Simple Syndication
See RSS
recording, audio file, 88–90
*Reference and Collection Development on
the Internet: A How-To-Do-It Manual
for Librarians* (Thomsen), 83
reference content, of Wiki, 45
research guide
Biz Wiki, challenges of, 52–54
Biz Wiki, content of, 45–47
Biz Wiki, organization/search
function, 47–49
need for change, 41–43
usage of Biz Wiki, 52

research guide *(cont'd.)*
  Wiki, setting up, 43–45
  Wiki as, 39–41, 54
resources
  Juice link, 85
  MediaWiki, 44
  PALINET Technology
    Conversations Podcast Series, xi
  podcast directories, 86
  RSS feed creation, 94
  RSS-to-Javascript Converter, 65
review, of library blog, 73–74
Rousseau, Tyler, x–xi, 83–97
RSS
  advantages of, 17, 18, 34–35
  future uses of, 33–34
  library blog and, 64
  readers, users and, 28–29
  RSS-to-Javascript Converter for
    blogs, 64–68
  technology overview, 1–2, 19
  users' knowledge of, 63–64
RSS Creator
  benefits of, 10–11
  challenges of, 11–12
  overview of, 5, 12–13
  RSS technology overview, 1–2
  three-step process, 5–10
  ToC alerts/journal feeds, problems
    with, 2–4
RSS feeds
  benefits of, 19–20
  blogging to courseware, 74
  database authentication, 32
  podcast RSS feed, creation of, 93–94
  podcasts, finding, 85–86
  podcasts and, 84
  publisher-supplied vs. RSS Creator,
    9–10
  subscription database, types of, 21–22
  for subscription databases, library
    application of, 30–32
  validation of, 94
  Web page integration of, 25–26

RSS generator, 93–94
RSS Search Alerts, 22–25
RSS-to-Javascript Converter, 64–68, 75

S
Schwartz, Greg, 94–95
search
  Internet search vs. "subscribe and
    filter", 28, 35
  for podcasts, 85–86
  research guide, 43
  RSS feed custom, 21–22
  Wiki search functions, 47–48
Search Alerts, RSS, 22–25
self-aggregation, 28–29
services
  See library services; RSS Creator
SFX Knowledgebase, 5, 11–12
SFX link resolver, 1–2
spam, 53–54
Steven Bell's Keeping Up Web site, 60
stopwords, 47–48
students
  library blog and, 69–71
  use of RSS feeds, 28
  Wiki community editing, 53–54
  Wiki updates and, 49–51
subject guides, 31
  See also research guide
subscription, library blog, 71
subscription databases
  See databases, subscription
survey
  on blogging knowledge, 63–64
  library blog, 70, 76–79

T
Table of Contents alerts, problems with,
  2–4
technology
  hype cycle, ix
  new, implementation of, 59, 60–62,
    75
Tenant, Roy, 29

Thomas Ford Memorial Library,
Illinois, 96
Thomsen, Elizabeth, 83
Thoreau, Henry David, 19
three-step process, RSS Creator
ISSN queries via Metalib X server,
7–8
MARC records upload, 5–6
SFX Knowledgebase download, 5
time, 73
traffic, library blog, 70

U
Uniform Resource Locator (URL),
65–66
updates
library blog, 72
research guide, 43
Wiki content, adding/editing,
49–52
Wiki for, 39, 41
usage, Wiki, 52
users
authentication, RSS feed database,
32–33
behavior, tracking, 34
blog to courseware and, 69–71
library blog and, 62–64, 72–73
new content notification and, 2–3
RSS and, 20
RSS Creator and, 6–7, 12
RSS readers and, 28–29
virtual reference and, 60–61

V
validation, of RSS feed, 94
virtual reference, 60–61

W
Walker, David, ix–x, 1–12
Web sites
RSS Creator and, 10–11
RSS feed integration, 25–26
RSS feeds and, 3–4, 31
RSS-to-Javascript Converter for
blogs, 64–68
Web-based subject guides, 39–43
See also Wiki
Western Kentucky University, podcasts
of, 96
Wiemer, Kris, 66
Wiki
Biz Wiki, challenges, 52–54
Biz Wiki, usage of, 52
Biz Wiki's content, 45–47
Biz Wiki's organization/search
features, 47–49
content, adding/editing, 49–52
function for library, 39–41
as research guide, 39, 54
research guides, need for change,
41–43
setting up, 43–45
Wikipedia, 43–44

Y
Yen, Tracy, 63

About the Editors

H. Frank Cervone is the Assistant University Librarian for Information Technology at Northwestern University. The author of four books in applied Information Technology, he also writes a regular column for *OCLC Systems and Services: International Digital Library Perspectives.* A well-known speaker on topics related to libraries and technology, he is a member of the NISO Metasearch Task Force and is the Chair of the CIC (Committee for Institutional Cooperation) Library Information Technology Directors as well as the Chair of the CARLI (Consortium of Academic and Research Libraries in Illinois) Learning Objects task force.

He holds an MSEd with a specialization in Online Teaching and Learning from California State University and an MA with a specialization in Information Technology Management in Information Agencies from DePaul University. Currently, he is a Ph.D. candidate in Management from Northcentral University.

Kathlene Hanson is LITA Acquisitions Editor and has worked as an academic librarian for 11 years. She has been Electronic Resources Coordinator at California State University, Monterey Bay Library for the past seven years. She has an MS in Library and Information Sciences from University of Illinois at Urbana-Champaign, an MA in Comparative Literature from State University New York at Binghamton, and BAs in English and German from Northern Illinois University.

3m